# Praise for
## *Ready or Not...They're Gay*

"Parents will easily identify with Paul and Hjordy. They welcome us into their lives and share with us the joys of having two gay sons. At times they fear for the safety of their sons and struggle to keep their family together; all the while emphasizing acceptance. We can all learn from their stories about the importance of unconditional love in a world that is oftentimes cruel to our gay, lesbian, bisexual and transgender loved ones."

—*Jody Huckaby, Executive Director, PFLAG National*

"Paul and Hjordy share an honest account of real stories and inspiring perspectives of experiences encountered over a ten-year span. This is a wonderful resource for parents, grandparents, and families when they discover their loved one is gay."

—*Deb LeMay, Representative of PFLAG St. Paul/Minneapolis*

"An engaging, personal, and charming book, *Ready or Not... They're Gay* is a tremendous resource, offering the views of different members of a single family. Highly recommended for parents seeking to understand their own situation and to better support their gay child."

—*Stephen White, The Rainbow Connection & San Diego Psychologist*

# READY OR NOT...
# THEY'RE GAY

Stories from a Midwestern Family

**Paul & Hjordy Wagner**

**Synergy Books**

*BOOK LAUNCH!*
*Paul N. Wagner*
*Hjordy Wagner*
*5-21-09*

Ready or Not...They're Gay: Stories from a Midwestern Family
Published by Synergy Books
P.O. Box 80107
Austin, Texas 78758

For more information about our books, please write to us, call 512.478.2028, or visit
our website at www.synergybooks.net.

Publisher's Cataloging-in-Publication
*(Provided by Quality Books, Inc.)*

Wagner, Paul, 1950-
     Ready or not-- they're gay : stories from a
Midwestern family / Paul & Hjordy Wagner. -- 1st ed.
     p. cm.
     LCCN 2008909350
     ISBN-13: 978-0-9815462-8-5
     ISBN-10: 0-9815462-8-5

     1. Wagner, Paul, 1950- 2. Wagner, Hjordy.
3. Parents of gays--United States. 4. Gays--Family
relationships--United States. 5. Coming out (Sexual
orientation)--United States. 6. Parent and child--
United States.   I. Wagner, Hjordy. II. Title.

HQ76.3.U5W34 2009          306.874
                    QBI08-600308

"Gay teens need role models," written by Hjordy and Paul Wagner, originally appeared
in the *Leader-Telegram* on April 12, 2008. Reprinted with permission of the *Leader-
Telegram*.

"It Seems to Me: Gay lifestyle just like everyone else's," written by Virginia Wolf,
originally appeared in the *Leader-Telegram* on August 8, 2008. Reprinted with
permission of Virginia Wolf and the *Leader-Telegram*.

Skip Petrie's letter reprinted with permission of his wife, Patricia Petrie. All other
contributed articles reprinted with permission of the authors.

Magazine and Photo Credits: *Instinct* Magazine for permission to reprint their front
cover design, including the photo from Joe Schmelzer, *Lavender* Magazine and Armour
Photography for permission to reprint their front cover photo, and Julie Gilbert, Best
Buy SVP Retail Training and Leadership Development and founder of WoLF (Women
Leaders Forum), for the reprint of the WoLF photo.

10 9 8 7 6 5 4 3 2 1

# Table of Contents

Preface ................................................................ ix

Acknowledgments ............................................... xi

Introduction ...................................................... xiii

## Part I: Memories from Mom

Ready or Not...I'm Gay: The first twenty-four hours ................. 1

Wise Ones ........................................................ 8

Error in Judgment ................................................ 10

Sisterhood ........................................................ 11

Our First Public Retelling of Our Story ....................... 13

Commitment Ceremony Hawaiian Style ....................... 15

Reception with the Happy Couple ............................ 17

A Letter to Brad from His Uncle .............................. 19

1999 Christmas Letter Excerpt ............................... 21

A Cousin But Never a Groomsman ............................ 23

Andrew's First Twenty-four Hours ............................ 25

Andrew Went Underground ................................... 28

Finally—An Explanation of "True" ............................ 32

Son Number Two Comes Out: A Christmas Letter .......... 33

Parents Open the Closet Door:
Telling family, friends and relatives ........................ 35

Boyfriends Are No Different Than Girlfriends ............... 37

Friends ........................................................... 39

The Massage Therapist Discloses Her Suspicions .......... 40

A *Will & Grace* Story: Ursula & Jürg ...................... 42

Eleven Years Later: Has there been a change? ............ 44

# Part II: Reflections from Dad

A Touch on the Shoulder .......................................................49

Paul's Top Ten List ............................................................. 51

10. Have an Open Mind ................................................. 52

9. Get Educated.......................................................... 58

8. Practice Tolerance................................................... 62

7. Don't Burn Bridges ................................................. 65

6. Be a Good Listener ................................................. 67

5. Be Nonjudgmental.................................................. 69

4. Pray ...................................................................... 72

3. Show Your Support on Issues ....................................74

2. Put Yourself in Their Shoes ...................................... 78

1. Look to the Future ................................................. 80

Why Write This Book? ........................................................ 83

# Part III: Brad, Andrew, and Grandma Say a Few Words

Over the Rainbow ..............................................................87

Family Bonds Triumph Over Everything................................. 92

Being a Grandparent Is a Great Experience..........................96

# Part IV: Tools for Navigating Your Own Story

Quotes We Live By............................................................. 101

Tips for Parents and Friends: How to
respond when a friend or loved one comes out.................... 103

Tips for Children: How to
have a positive coming out experience ............................... 104

What Can We Do in Our Schools? ..................................... 105

Checklist for Educators ...................................................... 108

Dear Abby Speaks Out...................................................... 110

Paul's Top Ten List............................................................. 111

What Is Your Story?........................................................... 112

## Part V: Stories from Others

Crystal Clear by Pastor Janet Ellinger .................................. 115

Not One but TWO! by Kay Peterson ................................. 117

My Sister Confided in Me by Judy Brase............................ 122

How I Found My Way to
a Loving Relationship by Cheryl Sutter .............................. 125

Connections Matter by Anonymous ................................... 141

Gay Lifestyle Just Like
Everyone Else's by Virginia Wolf...................................... 146

A Look at the Authors ........................................................149

# Preface

I was sitting in the nursing home in Plainview, Minnesota, with my eighty-eight-year-old father, Charlie. We talked about a lot of things that day. I thanked my dad for supporting our son. His response? "Of course we support him. Look at everything we would have missed if we hadn't." His words have stayed with my husband and me ever since that day; his words are the cornerstone of this book.

It has been twelve years since our oldest son, Bradley, told us he is gay. Five years later, his brother, Andrew, shared that he is gay as well. We embraced our sons' sexuality and were blessed with open-minded friends and family members who did so as well. However, we have heard many disturbing stories of young people who, after revealing they were homosexual, were abandoned by one or both parents, relatives, or friends. We have been encouraged by many people, including our sons, clergy, and friends, to share our story with the hope that by learning from our experiences, others will be better equipped to cope when they find out their son, daughter, brother, sister, niece, nephew, friend, or neighbor is gay. This is a mission for us—a mission that we hope will improve the relationships and lives of families and friends.

Other factors motivated us to write our story and share our recommendations. A recent Dear Abby letter spoke about a young man who committed suicide because he couldn't bring himself to tell his parents he was gay. In looking at the statistics of teenage suicides, we found a 1989 study conducted by the Department of Health and Human Services (HHS) that found that gay youth are two to three times more likely to attempt suicide than other young people and comprise up to 30 percent of suicides annually. We were astounded by this information. My husband and I looked at one another and said, "Yet another reason to write our story." There is more information about the HHS published report in part IV.

Another story we summarized was about a staff member in the workplace who resisted telling her students that she was a lesbian even though her students asked her year after year if that was the case. Our position? We can no longer ask gay teachers and gay children to hide in the closet because they are afraid of harassment, bullying, or job security. We have more detail on that incident in part IV.

We cannot stand by and watch our children be bullied by other children because they are gay. We can no longer have educators stand on the sideline observing this kind of behavior from their students. We have incidents and comments on bullying in parts II and IV, and a special narrative in part V.

These are but a few of the reasons we are recording our stories and the stories from others. Too many bad things are happening to homosexual children and those who love them most. We hope you enjoy the light-hearted moments we have offered, take with you the recommendations for families and educators that fit your situation, and savor the heartfelt stories from our sons, their grandma, and our friends.

—*Hjordy*

# Acknowledgments

There are many people who deserve acknowledgment for their help and support during the process of writing this book. There are still more who have touched our lives and given us courage and strength when we needed it most. And last of all, we are extremely grateful to our contributing authors who risked telling their stories in our book: Kay Peterson, Cheryl Sutter, Jude Brase, Janet Ellinger, Virginia Wolf, our anonymous author, and "Grandma" Audrey Christison.

There is one person, however, whom we want to honor in this book who hasn't had a chance to tell his story, share his life with a loved one, or read this book. He tragically took his life during his college years. He was so desperate in his inner struggle that in January 1974 he couldn't live long enough to see his beloved Vikings play in the Super Bowl. Look at all he, his family, and friends missed because of the pain he felt he could not live with any longer.

He was a friend to all, an enemy to no one. Big V was and will always be a true buddy of ours. Hjordy and I both hold him in our hearts, and we hope this book will make it easier for young people and their families who have struggles that may seem insurmountable to find their way to each other.

—*Paul and Hjordy*

# Introduction

My wife, Hjordy, and I were both raised in small Minnesota communities. My hometown is Caledonia, and Hjordy grew up in rural Plainview. Both towns were farming communities. I was a "city slicker," and Hjordy was raised on a farm. Both of our families had many relatives living in or near our towns. We lived with our families for our first eighteen years, and our upbringings were very similar. Everything was centered around family, church, school, sports, and friends. I met Hjordy during my junior year at Winona State College. Our relationship grew, and we were married one year after college. We settled in Eau Claire, Wisconsin. Both of us were hired by the school district and had lifelong careers in education. Recently we retired after more than thirty years of teaching children and working in district-related jobs.

Our children were born in 1977 and 1982. Brad is five years older than Andrew. Each boy lived at home until his eighteenth birthday. Church, school, sports, and friends were a major focus during their formative years. The setting for our family was not exactly *Leave it to Beaver*, but it was a typical "American Dream" script of that era: mom, dad, two children, a dog, and a two-car garage.

Hjordy and I are about as down to earth as can be. We have supported each other and our boys throughout our marriage. Nothing in our family life has changed since our two boys told us that they are gay. If anything, we are more united as a family. We cherish every moment that we spend with our sons and their partners.

We hope this short overview of our family has given you a better idea of our life before we met each other and the history created after we met on that memorable Valentine's Day in 1970.

*—Paul and Hjordy*

# PART I

## Memories from Mom

# Ready or Not...I'm Gay:
## The first twenty-four hours

*"The very first thought that crossed my mind
was that my next words were going to be
remembered for the rest of our lives."*

There are days that will always remain in your memory in a crystal-clear state. October 29, 1996, was that day for our family; a day that changed our lives.

Our oldest son, Brad, arrived home from teaching a fitness class at the Athletic Club. Our fourteen-year-old son, Andrew, was in the process of receiving a lecture about the importance of telling the truth. It was the standard parent lecture: "You may still find yourself in trouble, but you'll be in a lot more trouble if you don't tell the truth. You have to be very smart to not get caught up in lies, blah, blah, blah." We had a lot of different ways of reminding the kids of this simple truth. Hearing the lecture must have stirred an emotion in Brad.

When my lecture wound down, Brad said, "Mom, I'm going to take a shower. When I get done, would you please come downstairs? I need to talk to you about something. Come alone." I got the churning stomach sensation all parents get when they know that there is something big on their child's mind. As parents, we always wonder if we will have the right demeanor and advice when those defining moments confront us.

I put Andrew to bed, and Paul was already turning in for the evening. I went downstairs and waited.

The shower stopped. I waited.

After about ten minutes, Brad nestled into the couch and started to tell me what was on his mind. I have paraphrased, as best as I can remember, this heart-wrenching talk.

Brad was curled up on the sectional couch about two feet from where I was sitting. He cleared his throat several times before he spoke. "Mom, I listened to your lecture about lying that you gave to Andrew. I guess I have been living a lie for many years. In fact, my whole life has been a lie." There was a pause as he appeared to be groping for the next words. "It is time I told you the truth." His statement made me uncomfortable yet anxious to hear what he had been hiding.

"This is hard for me to tell you, so I guess I am just going to say it. I am gay." At that moment, I felt like I was having an out-of-body experience. I saw myself above the couch looking down on the two of us. The very first thought that crossed my mind was that my next words were going to be remembered for the rest of our lives. I paused and thought. I am sure it may have seemed like an eternity to Brad, but it was probably only five seconds or so.

"Brad, you've caught me off guard on this. I guess the first thing that comes to my mind is, how do you know that you are gay?"

"I have always known I was different from other boys. Just like you knew you were attracted to Dad and other guys in your life, I knew I was attracted to males. I have just always known." He paused, waiting for a response. When I didn't have any words, he continued. "I went to see Janet (a pastor at the United Methodist Church) about this, Mom. She really helped me to get ready for this moment with you."

"You went to see Janet? I am glad she was there for you. What did she say to help you?"

"She said that God loves you and loves everything about you; trust in that love; believe in that love."

"What about dating Katie? How come you went out with her when you knew there was nowhere to go with that?"

"I guess it was a cover-up. I like Katie as a friend. Mom, I know you have a lot of questions. It took me a long time to figure out who I was and become comfortable with who I am. I know this is going to take you some time, and I will help you and Dad. You can ask me any question you want. I will help in any way that I can."

My head was swirling. I felt like Brad was the parent and I was the child. His words were comforting and so mature.

"You know how hard this is to tell you. I thought about this moment for a long time. Sometimes I was so confused about who I was and how to tell you and others about my attraction to men that I thought about committing suicide. This has been hard, but I am ready now to be honest and face who I am."

That comment about suicide hit me like a bolt of lightning. No parent wants to believe their child would ever entertain the thought of suicide. That was one of the saddest comments I heard from Brad. How many kids felt that suicide was their only alternative? It scared and saddened me. I knew then that there was nothing more important than his safety in being able to be himself. No more lies and no more hiding.

"Brad, I feel so bad that you felt so alone and couldn't share this with us. I don't know what I would have done if something would have happened to you. I hope you know that you can always come to your father and me with anything. There is nothing you can do that could change our love for you."

"I had talks...with Brandy."—our dog—"If Brandy could talk, she would have a lot of stories to tell about me."

I heard a noise by the staircase followed by crying. It was Andrew. "Brad, I have to go talk to Andrew, I think he was listening." I went quickly up the stairs only to meet Paul coming out of the bedroom. "What is going on around here?"

"Paul, go down and talk with Brad. Please be calm. I have to stay with Andrew for a little bit." Paul looked at me totally confused. I felt bad that we couldn't be together at that moment, but I knew Andrew needed someone with him. Paul walked downstairs, and I went into Andrew's bedroom.

He was facedown on his bed, sobbing. He had obviously overheard our conversation. I rubbed his back and tried to comfort him. "Andrew, I am sorry this upsets you." His next words have stayed with me to this day and five years later came back to me in a most memorable way.

"Don't worry, Mom, I will have three, four, five babies to make up for the babies Brad won't have." It was an unexpected remark. He was worried about us; he was worried about our future as grandparents. Who would have guessed that would be the first thing out of his mouth?

"Andrew, you are not responsible for making up for Brad. You don't have babies for grandparents. You have them because you want to have a baby. You know, Andrew, it doesn't matter if Dad and I never have grandchildren. That is your choice; that is Brad's choice. It doesn't matter if you never have children, and it doesn't matter if you are gay. We aren't disappointed in Brad, and we won't be disappointed if you and Brad don't have children, gay or not."

I rubbed his back a little longer, and he eventually stopped crying. I told him to try to get some sleep and we would talk in the morning.

I went downstairs to see how Brad and his father were doing. When I came down, I heard for the first time that Brad intended to leave town and move to Minneapolis. Everything was moving way too fast for me. Paul looked stunned.

"My friends told me that I should have money in the bank and be ready to be kicked out of my house. I've already figured everything out. I will be happier in Minneapolis than in Eau Claire."

"Maybe that is what you should do." Paul's response sounded harsh, but he later explained that he thought it would be an easier life in Minneapolis. Eau Claire isn't a small town, but it is conservative. Minneapolis is a magnet community, full of diverse people and ideas. At that time, we didn't understand that Minneapolis-St. Paul was gay-friendly, but that was one of many things that Brad taught us along the way.

"Dad, I told this to Mom. I will answer any question that you have. It took me a long time to figure this out, and it will take you a long time to understand and accept this. I want to help you."

"Of course, we are afraid of AIDS, Brad. Are you well educated about protecting yourself?" Paul's question had also been on my mind. Apparently it was a concern from both of us, especially at that particular time, when everywhere you turned there was another article or news story talking about the AIDS epidemic. And in our limited experience, it seemed that AIDS was associated with gay men, so the red flag was raised in our minds.

"Yes, I had a great health teacher. I know how to protect myself." That was one of many questions that were yet to come. My biggest question was why he couldn't tell us. I'm still not sure why kids don't tell their parents when they suspect something. It is, however, uncommon for children to tell their parents during their high school years. We also learned that some gays and lesbians shield their family into adulthood; some people never tell their parents.

We hugged Brad and went to bed. Sleep was not a viable choice. I didn't shed a tear when we were with Brad, but the tears came as soon as the bedroom door closed. I think I cried all night. As I reflect on that night now, I believe this was the first step of the mourning process. I had to let go of our vision of what we believed about our son and what we thought was in his future. During that first night, my thoughts were fear—fear of his future, fear of what others would think, fear of harassment, fear of my own feelings. Paul turned one way in bed, and I turned the other way. It was a night in which we fought our own demons by ourselves.

The night and day blurred together. I didn't sleep and wanted to stay home, but I had to facilitate a meeting in the morning and had a presentation to give in the afternoon. I looked in the mirror at my red, puffy eyes and wondered how I would make it through the day.

Before I left for the day, Brad came upstairs from his bedroom on the lower level of our home. He asked how I slept. I told him it was a sleepless night. I asked him how he slept. "Mom, I slept the best I have slept in years—like a baby."

I am not sure how I made it through the morning. When I came into the office, my secretary knew there was something wrong. "Hjordy, are you okay?"

"I really can't talk about it right now." I knew if I said more, the tears would flow again. She accepted my answer. About fifteen minutes later, she came back in. "I'm worried about you. You aren't ill, are you?"

"I am sorry for worrying you. No, I am not ill."

"Thank goodness, you scared me. If you feel like talking, let me know."

I wasn't ready to talk to her just yet, but I knew when I was she could be trusted and would be supportive of me.

I went to my afternoon presentation. My eyes looked like I either had a severe infection or had been crying all day. The principal noticed immediately and asked if I was okay. She volunteered to give the presentation for me. I told her I would get through it.

Once I was done, I was approached by a longtime friend who asked me what was wrong. I couldn't hold it in any longer. The tears started again. We went into her office, and I blurted it out to her. She was the first person I spoke with about our recent news. Surprisingly, she had a roommate who was a lesbian. I was blessed to be with a person who was nonjudgmental and whose words were comforting to me. I regained my composure and headed home. I couldn't wait to be in the quiet of my home to finally start sorting through the many things that were on my mind. I made my first phone call to Ted, my brother-in-law, who was a minister and a counselor. I needed his pastoral guidance as well as his clinical advice.

Ted was a great comfort to me. He knew I was struggling with a lot of issues. We talked about young men who thought they were homosexuals, the help available to them, and about young men who were born homosexuals. We also discussed Brad's spiritual health as a gay man. I felt reassured that Brad, as with all of God's children, is loved and supported by his Lord.

Paul and I aren't going to spend significant time in this book on the religious debate regarding homosexuals. We worked through our questions and are comfortable with our belief. The more important issue for us was our commitment to love and support our child just as God loves and supports us. We know this is an issue that most parents, aunts, uncles, grandparents, and friends will need to work through, and we encourage you to seek answers to your questions.

I started my recovery process after my talk with Ted. I had a long way to go, but I turned a small corner that night. Paul and I had several more questions for Brad that night. We could tell a load had been lifted from his shoulders; he was very happy. He was making plans to tell some other key people. He was confident about who he was and what his next steps would be.

My next plan was to find a book. I went to a local bookstore and found a book that I thought would be helpful. It made a world of difference to both of us. That is another reason we wanted to write this book. It is a payback to others who may need encouragement and answers during this huge transition time.

# Wise Ones

*"The lesson we learned that day is to not make assumptions about how people will react—they will surprise you."*

Why were my parents the last to be told about Brad? It seems silly now as we reflect on the day. We knew that my mom and dad held a sacred covenant of unconditional love for their family. I remember repeating their strong-held philosophy to our children: "We love you when you're good, we love you when you're bad, we love you all the time." Even though that was a childhood verse, our sons knew there was nothing they could do that would alter our love for them. Their grandparents demonstrated that love for us and their grandchild in a most memorable way.

We often lingered after breakfast to spread out our conversation about politics, recent jokes and stories, and general chitchat about life in general. We always enjoyed this time with my mom and dad. It was fun to hear their stories and share our stories with them. That day Paul and I had a story to tell them; it was time to tell the truth about Brad.

They hung on every word we said. My mom and dad have always been very good listeners. When we finished with the general review of our last month, my mom said that she loved Brad and that would never change. She also shared that she often wondered if he was gay. My father was thoughtful and then said one and one thing only: "Who are we to pass judgment—how do we know that Jesus wasn't gay? You know, there was never a reference to a woman in his life."

We are still in awe of Dad's statement, but not for the reason you may think. It was his voice of support for Brad and for us. Neither one of them have wavered since that day. In fact, they have been advocates. My mom was so upset with the Methodist Church's stand on gays, she wrote a letter expressing her displeasure with their position. The lesson we learned that day is to not make assumptions about how people will react—they will surprise you. Sometimes the surprise is pleasant, and sometimes you expect support and don't get it.

# Error in Judgment

*"I can only imagine how the incident influenced his
sense of how my niece felt about homosexuality."*

Andrew was invited to stay with our niece. He always enjoyed
spending time with her because she was fun and he loved playing
with her kids. After Andrew returned home, she called us and said
we might want to talk with Andrew because he seemed upset about
Brad's latest announcement. She informed me that she watched a
videotape with Andrew that her mom had sent her about the issue
of being gay. She said she had asked him if he wanted to see the tape
with her, and he had agreed to.

After I talked with my niece, I asked Andrew what the tape contained. He said it was a religious tape about being gay. I then knew
why our son was upset. As I reflect back on the incident today, it
also concerns me that he was shown the tape when, at that time, he
was internalizing his own sexuality and how some people might feel
about him and his brother. Both of our boys are spiritual; they pray
every day and take their spirituality seriously. I can only imagine how
the incident influenced his sense of how my niece felt about homosexuality as well as how others might feel in the future. He was only
in middle school at the time.

Andrew's cousin probably thought she was helping, and she probably thought Andrew could handle it. Both boys have and always
will adore their cousin, but I believe the decision to show the video
was an error in judgment on her part.

# Sisterhood

*"You hear stories about gays and lesbians 'coming out,' but you don't often hear stories about 'parents coming out.'"*

Every year, the Wagner girls—my sister-in-laws, niece, and our nephews' wives—meet for a weekend to do our Christmas shopping. It is a valued weekend with deep traditions and as revered as the hunting season is to a deer hunter.

The 1996 shopping trip was one week after Brad shared his truth. He wanted me to tell his aunts and cousins his news. Our plan was to personally discuss this with our immediate family members. I was still emotionally fragile, but I knew this was the opportune time to talk with them. Still, I was nervous. I didn't look forward to our Saturday-night talk.

It was a typical weekend: we ate at our favorite restaurants, talked, and shopped. We had our traditional relaxation time on Saturday night where we caught up on everyone's life and family, shared the events of the day, and claimed bragging rights to our great buys. My niece was pampering me with a pedicure. I knew I had to tell them soon or they would slowly drift off to their respective sleeping quarters—floor, sleeping bag, and couch.

I nervously took the stage and reviewed the events of our last week. The reaction was warm and supportive. What I didn't expect was the floodgate of other issues that erupted; confessions breed confessions. Henceforth it was a night of unconditional support by my "sisters," not only for me, but for others who shared some of their

11

own turmoil and fears. As our discussion drew to a close, I entrusted them to go back to their families and deliver the news. I knew I was giving them a difficult task, but I couldn't go to each and every person in the family. I knew they would handle it in a loving and compassionate way.

I realized that evening how difficult this had to be for Brad and Andrew over their many years of keeping this secret and then finally telling those they love most the truth about the "hidden" part of each of them that they had never shared. You hear stories about gays and lesbians "coming out," but you don't often hear stories about "parents coming out." Unfortunately, some parents keep this information deeply hidden behind the doors of their home. We've met some of the children of those families. We have the distinct impression that support of these children is also deeply hidden.

# Our First Public
## Retelling of Our Story

---

*"I had a debate with myself for a while but finally decided that no one can argue with our story—it is our story."*

---

My sister-in-law was taking a diversity class at the University of Wisconsin-La Crosse. Her classmates ranged from undergraduate students to practicing educators. She had shared some of her learning with us during the early part of the semester. The class had an upcoming evening devoted to homosexuals that was to be hosted by guest speakers. The usual speakers for the event were college-age gays and lesbians. However, the professor had exhausted his list of regular speakers. Everyone was unavailable on that particular evening. My sister-in-law told her professor she had someone in mind.

I was a little reluctant to accept the invitation. I had never spoken publicly about our story. I wasn't sure if my emotions were stable enough to share with an audience. Would they be friendly, or would I have skeptics? I just wasn't sure if I had what it took to do a good job. I had a debate with myself for a while but finally decided that no one can argue with our story—it is our story. My sister-in-law is persuasive, and I finally accepted the challenge.

I sat in the audience as the professor covered some interesting material about homosexuals. I cannot repeat with accuracy what he said now, but I remember being fascinated by his lecture. The last part of the class was all devoted to me. I wasn't sure what they wanted, so I just started telling our story.

I scanned the audience and observed there were men and women of a variety of age groups, which I have since learned doesn't necessarily give you clues as to their position on homosexuality. It was a bit emotional at times for me, but I was able to get through it without a breakdown. I tried to read the audience as I was talking. They were very attentive—you could have heard a pin drop. Other than that, I couldn't tell how I was doing by their facial expressions.

There were several respectful questions from the audience, which I was able to answer. My surprise came after the lecture. Several people in the class thanked me for coming and said they appreciated hearing a parent perspective. That was a landmark evening for me. Up until that point, I had never spoken with adults outside of family and friends about Brad. I had certainly not spoken with a group of people who may or may not have appreciated my story or point of view. I felt that if I was called upon to do something like this again, I could do it with confidence. I also felt I gave them something important that evening. I gave them a piece of my soul that had been hidden from everyone except our most trusted friends and family. I felt liberated.

Paul's sister called upon us once again about eight years later. This time we were in front of her teaching peers, who were taking a class on diversity. Paul and I combined our efforts and shared our story. We also added some learning we have observed about the school setting and the importance of modeling "diverse speech and actions." We handed out a few of our chapters. It was an interesting reaction—most wanted to edit our work! True teachers.

Paul and I are very grateful to his sister and her husband for their unconditional support. They have never wavered in their actions or voice regarding our two boys.

# Commitment Ceremony
# Hawaiian Style

*"It was no different than a heterosexual wedding in
its commitment, passion, and romance."*

Brad and his partner approached us with the idea of a commitment ceremony in Hawaii. It took us about ten seconds to say yes. Brad made all the arrangements. We booked some time-shares, and we had a trip of a lifetime planned for August 1999.

Paul and I vacationed the first week in Waikiki. We had fun touring the island and exploring this exciting part of the United States. The second week we had a time-share booked in Kauai. We got settled in our condo and familiarized ourselves with the area so we were ready to meet Andrew, Brad, and Brad's partner at the airport. They arrived two days before their commitment ceremony. In that time, we explored the island and enjoyed each other's company. We were all relaxed and in a vacation mode.

The afternoon of the ceremony was a perfect setting for a romantic commitment ceremony. The sun was about forty-five minutes away from setting. We listened to their loving words to one another, took photos and video, and after the sun set, moved to the part of the beach where we had our dinner. The setting was perfect. We were enclosed in a tent with the backdrop of water lightly splashing onto the shoreline. We took off our shoes and dug our toes in the cool sand.

The dinner was the most memorable dining experience I have ever had. Each of the four courses was delivered from Princeville's hotel, which was at least four flights of steps away. We savored every bite of food. The entrees were all delicious, but the crab cakes, especially, were the best I can ever remember tasting. The end of the evening was complete when the wedding cake was cut. It was not only a symbol of Brad and Chad's union but it was absolutely delicious!

In between each course, we took turns asking our "dinner questions." This was and has been a tradition in our family. We think of a question that requires some thought and exposes a little more about each of us. For example, "Describe your life ten years from now," or "What have you done that gives you great pride in yourself?" Their dreams of their future were no different than any other young couple. They talked about their pride in their work and what they hoped to achieve in the future. They talked about having a home they can both enjoy. The same things any heterosexual couple might discuss at this time in their life.

It was a sterling evening. None of us wanted it to end. It was and is what every family dreams about for their children on their wedding day. This is the feeling every family with a gay child should feel. It was no different than a heterosexual wedding in its commitment, passion, and romance. It couldn't have been a better experience and remains as one of our most memorable moments. We love Chad and always will. He became our third son that night. As my husband has said since, "We have four gay sons, and we love all of them as our own." Who could ever see the wrong in that?

# Reception with the Happy Couple

*"As I looked around, I started to notice that
our family members were disappearing one
by one, family by family."*

The commitment ceremony was followed by a reception a few months later in a downtown Minneapolis business. As you looked outside of the second-story window, you saw the lights and skyline of the beautiful city. The tables were set to perfection with flowers from Hawaii. Name tags were on each table along with honored seating at the head table. It was no different than walking into a wedding reception for any other wedded couple.

Brad and his partner were dressed for the event in their tuxedos. They could not have looked more handsome. Paul, Andrew, and I had our night attire of black and white. Andrew was very proud to be Brad's best man. The evening started out with hors d'oeuvres and beverages. Prior to dinner being served, I gave the prayer on behalf of both families. Dinner was served following the early reception. Since the traditional "wedding" cake was served in Hawaii, they had ordered a variety of small desserts that the guests could choose from at the dessert table. It was truly a hit. As the dinner and desserts were enjoyed by all, Paul and I made our way around the tables to greet all the guests. This was the first time that most of the guests had ever attended a commitment reception for a gay couple. We were received by each table with compliments on our son and his partner. They also commented on the support and tastefulness of the event.

A short program followed dinner. They showed the video of their commitment ceremony. There were tears and laughter as we all watched this special moment between two young men who loved each other. Andrew spoke on behalf of his brother and his partner, and there were other nice comments made by friends. The night would not have been complete without the dancing. The "mother's dance" was the first dance; after that, everyone jumped onto the dance floor.

As I looked around, I started to notice that our family members were disappearing one by one, family by family. It puzzled me that they were not staying until the end. We had always closed the doors at every family wedding dance, yet family members were trickling out. That is when we realized that, as great as it was that most of the family had come to the reception, it was not viewed as a wedding celebration. They probably came more out of an obligation to family than out of a true feeling of joy. Regardless of their reasons, that is how we felt at the end of the evening. I was heartsick about that and have been ever since. There are times yet that I get emotional about why the most normal of things for our boys is so hard for others. Brad continues to remind us that it is not our job to change people. We have to accept them for who they are and go from there. For the most part, Paul and I have respected his advice and have tried to live by that. That night, however, I was reminded of how much further ahead we were in our thinking and how far behind most of our family members still were.

# A Letter to **Brad from His Uncle**

*"We respected his honesty. 'Behind closed door' discussions that circle back to you hurt more."*

We received a copy of a letter that was sent to Brad from one of his uncles. I know that he gave the invitation to the reception great thought, to the point that he visited his priest. We know he loved Brad but just couldn't bring himself to attend the celebration of two young men who wanted to commit themselves to each for the rest of their lives. Unfortunately we lost Skip a few years later. We think in time he may have come to understand that which was foreign to him, but we will never have the chance to see that change occur. We have transcribed the letter just as he wrote it. None of us felt differently about Skip after reading the letter. In fact, we respected his honesty. "Behind closed door" discussions that circle back to you hurt more.

Sept 19, 1999

Dear Brad,

I'm writing to inform you of my not coming to your reception. I love you like all of the members of the family, I just can not accept your life style in my heart. I have talked to my parish Priest and he simply said if you do not accept that style of life, do not go and condone it. That is my choice. I have nothing against you or Chad let me make that clear. I do not care if you want to live together. I hope I do not hurt your mom and dad with my decision; they have always been there when I needed them. You are welcome at my home at any time. If you need help feel free to call—I'll try to help when and where I can.

Love,

Skip

*cc Paul and Hjordy*

# 1999 Christmas Letter Excerpt

---

*"Brad was joined with his lifetime partner, Chad, in a beautiful beachfront ceremony on August 9th."*

---

Every year we sent out a Christmas letter to family and friends. We have included the 1999 excerpt about Brad.

Dear Friends and Family:

Our news to you is usually pretty balanced between our family members and our extended family. This year, however, our boys took center stage.

In August our family journeyed to Hawaii. Paul and Hjordy took a "second honeymoon" the first week. The only way to describe our time in Hawaii is outstanding. It is better than we had imagined. Everywhere we went on the islands was beautiful.

The second week we were joined by the rest of the family for a very special event. Brad was joined with his lifetime partner, Chad, in a beautiful beachfront ceremony on August 9th. It was a backdrop shared by visitors and moviegoers from all over the world—a perfect setting for a wonderful event. We completed the evening with a candlelight dinner on the banks of the ocean. The second half of the celebration occurred on October 2nd in Minneapolis. We had an evening dinner followed by the video of the ceremony. The celebration would not have been complete without dancing. It was a memorable evening!

December 10, 1999

# A Cousin But **Never a Groomsman**

*"I pledged from that day on that things like that
would not interrupt our family again."*

Weddings in the Wagner family are big events. Paul has four siblings, one niece, and nine nephews. As time goes on, the next generation of babies is adding volume to our family. It is a joyful time for us because we can enjoy their wonderful children without having the day-to-day care of them. But first, let's talk about marriage.

The Wagner family met at the church for the wedding ceremony of one of Brad's cousins. Brad brought his partner along for the event. He was new to the family, so not many of the relatives knew much about him. At the conclusion of the service we went through the greeting line and were talking outside of the church. Brad informed me that he and his partner weren't going to attend the reception. I was puzzled as to why they had a change of heart. I vigorously questioned him about this turn of events. I wasn't buying his answer but proceeded to take Paul and Andrew to the reception and then drove Brad and Chad thirty miles back home to deliver them to their automobile. Still not satisfied with their answers, I continued to question their decision. Nothing more was shared with me at that time.

After dropping them off, I cried all the way back to the reception. Why couldn't I have my family together at a family wedding? What made them so uncomfortable? Everyone else had their loved ones together, but for some reason Brad felt he couldn't stay. My feelings spilled into the next day. I was, of course, happy for the bride and groom but sad for my son and his partner and for Paul, Andrew, and me. I was relieved to have the next-day present opening over so I could go home and not be reminded of what our family lost that weekend.

Several years later I asked Brad about that decision to leave. He reluctantly admitted that it was an uncomfortable situation for them. He said it was probably too soon for him to come with his partner. He also felt bad that he had never been asked by any of his cousins to be a part of a wedding party. He was quite sure he knew the reason. I feel bad to this day about their feeling of "outsidedness" at that wedding. I pledged from that day on that things like that would not interrupt our family again. Little did I know that more hurt was still ahead for us at another family gathering many years later.

# Andrew's First Twenty-four Hours

*"They used the term "fag hag." I asked Brad what that meant. His response would reveal yet another hidden truth in our family."*

Two years after the Christmas of Brad's ceremony, we gathered for a happy Thanksgiving. We picked up my parents to go to Brad's house for Thanksgiving dinner. It was a big outing for my mom and dad, as they don't travel long distances very often. I guess they couldn't refuse the invitation from Brad and his partner for Thanksgiving Day.

We had a wonderful dinner prepared by the boys. It was a treat for me not to be the major cook. It was a perfect day.

After dinner, we took mom and dad to their hotel for the evening. Then, we all settled in after the busy day to watch *Will and Grace*. The show brought its usual laughs and chuckles. Paul and I knew much of the humor went over our heads, but we still enjoyed the show. More than halfway into the show, they used the term *"fag hag."* I asked Brad what that meant. His response would reveal yet another hidden truth in our family.

"That would be like Jill loving me as a boyfriend even though she knows I'm gay, or like Becky loving Andrew." I asked him what he meant by that. He said, "Nothing, I was just using that as an example." There was dead silence, and at that point I knew a big secret had just been revealed. My stomach was queasy. I listened for Andrew's fun and easy laugh through the rest of the show. He didn't laugh anymore. That was an even bigger clue. Brad had once told me that you should never force a "coming out." It was advice I had given to another parent faced with the potential knowledge that her son was gay. I knew I had to leave it alone until Andrew was ready.

Paul and I said we were going to get ready for bed. We went upstairs and Brad followed. I asked him again about the remark. He tried to redeem himself, but inside I knew our second son was gay. Within five minutes, Brad came back up and asked Paul and me to go downstairs. Andrew wanted to talk with us.

Brad led the way. I hadn't talked to Paul about what happened during *Will and Grace*. I wasn't sure if he had picked up on the dialogue or not. It was like an old tape running through except the players were turned around. This time we were much better equipped to handle the news.

"You probably know what this is about. Brad let the news out during the show. You have another gay son." Andrew squirmed in his chair and followed up with a nervous question. "You kind of knew, didn't you?" His look told me he was hoping that we knew and were prepared for this moment. He was asking for reassurance that it was okay that he was gay. Andrew was partially right. Paul and I had discussed the possibility that Andrew was gay. In fact, a good friend told me that his classmates had suspected Andrew was gay. She told me the clues, and it got me thinking. Even though Paul and I had some thoughts about it, we hadn't decided if it was true or not. Even though we had been through this once and had five years under our belt, it still gave me a jolt.

Andrew came over and put his head in my lap and wrapped his arms around my legs and said, "Mom, I'm sorry that I won't have those kids like I said I would." That brought tears to his eyes and to mine. I wasn't sad about not having grandchildren; I was sad he had carried that burden with him for all that time. But now, I was more perplexed than ever that he made that promise five years ago, when he said he would have more children to make up for any Brad didn't have. Why did he feel that grandchildren were such an important factor in our life? I still don't know why this was such a critical issues to him then and now. I guess he must have really wanted us to be grandparents!

We talked some more. He wasn't ready to have us share the news with anyone else yet. We told him it was his call and he just needed to tell us how and when. We would follow his lead. He seemed relieved, and we gave him a hug and kissed him good night. Brad followed us upstairs and told us how proud he was of us. He said every gay person would love to have such supportive parents.

I can't say I slept soundly, but I did get some sleep. Paul was still in a fog about the *"fag hag"* remark. We laugh about that to this day. It went right over his head.

We went to get my mom and dad in the morning, and we hit the road to take them back home. I felt a little empty throughout the ride back to my hometown. I needed to talk about this, and I couldn't because Andrew had asked us not to tell anyone just yet. Because I was holding everything in, I ended up with a huge headache. We dropped mom and dad off, and we headed back home. I was grateful to talk with Paul and let out my emotions. Paul was very calm and appeared to be completely unaffected by the news. I was disappointed in myself that it took me a little longer to work through it.

# Andrew Went Underground

> *"If mom and dad are concentrating on
> Brad, maybe they will leave me alone."*

We haven't written as much about Andrew because Brad was the trailblazer in so much of our own personal growth. I don't know if it is common that the second gay son goes underground deeper than his brother, but that seemed to be the case in our family. Andrew, however, played detective on many occasions, which, as we look back now, appeared to be attempts to "out" his brother. The added benefit might have been to distract us from who he was: *If mom and dad are concentrating on Brad, maybe they will leave me alone.*

## Andrew—the investigator of Brad

During his freshman year in college, Brad was corresponding with a man in Iowa. They talked on the phone often, and guess who was listening? Andrew came to us and quoted one of the comments Brad said to this man: "I feel like I'm talking to myself." That alone didn't raise a huge flag, but other encounters with the man should have. He wanted Brad to visit Las Vegas with him, come live in his town, go to the local college, and many other interesting invitations. Brad did none of the above. He received a gift package from the man with a Vegas towel and other souvenirs that the man bought for Brad when he went to Las Vegas. Brad finally decided to visit this man and investigate the school. He came back totally uninterested in the school or in the man. He said the man was strange. We were happy that was the end of that. That was a huge clue. I am guessing that our conscious minds didn't want it to be so. In fact, it could have been a clue about Andrew, but he wasn't even on the radar.

Andrew also traced Brad's movements on the Internet. If you visit a gay web site, various unsolicited web sites appear on your computer. Andrew showed them to us, and we had a talk with Brad. He quickly skimmed over it and said he had no idea how it happened. We simply said that he had to make sure it didn't happen again as his brother should not see what was appearing on the screen. We asked Brad if something was going on, but he assured us that there was nothing. Andrew recognized the clues, acknowledged them, and tried to get us to see them, but we obviously didn't want to face the facts.

## Andrew playing the straight guy

Andrew is a desirable young man. He is good-looking, fun, athletic, and of solid intelligence. He dated one girl his freshman year. She was a very nice young lady, and as with most parents, we thought the dating game had started. It ended quite soon after it started. Andrew never dated again, but he did attend major dances with a girl just as his brother had done during his high school years. He mentioned one day that if he had "time to date," he would go out with this one young lady in the neighborhood. I hounded him a bit about that, as she was a very nice girl. He continued to say he didn't have time. He was busy with school and sports. My response was that other boys found time to date. Why couldn't he?

## Andrew and his secret boyfriends

We trusted both of our boys. They gave us no reason to distrust them. Andrew loves to dance, and he frequently went to a dance club in Menomonie, which is about twenty-five miles from Eau Claire. We heard about the friends he met and how much fun he had at the dance club. Little did we know that he also ventured farther west to clubs in the Twin Cities. We also didn't know that he had two boyfriends during that period of time. He pulled this off without a clue on our part. He was very clever.

Another incident happened during his senior swim season. Andrew, like Brad, was an extremely talented athlete. Both boys were swimmers and tennis players. Andrew told us he was feeling a lot of pressure his senior year, and we noticed he wasn't his usual self. We were concerned about him, so I stopped the swim coach one day and asked him if he had any insight into Andrew's lack of enthusiasm for swimming. He said Andrew broke down crying recently and that he thought something was going on. He suggested we talk with him. Andrew was stoic and continued to reassure us that he was okay. We attended the annual state championship swim meet in Madison. It was Andrew's last swim of his high school career. He didn't swim to his capabilities that day, and years later we found out why—he had broken up with his boyfriend.

## Andrew forsakes money for a large university

Andrew was on track for a swimming scholarship. Until March of his senior year, we thought we would have help with his college education. One day that all changed. He asked us not to be angry with him, but he really didn't want to swim anymore. He wanted to go to the University of Minnesota instead. After we got over the shock of the announcement, his dad and I talked it over. We weren't financially prepared for this decision, were shocked by the sudden turn of events, and we needed time to rethink our plan. Andrew hadn't even applied to the University of Minnesota. It all turned out in the end, but it was one of the surprises along the way. I am guessing he had a boyfriend in the cities or knew that the potential to find someone in Minneapolis was more possible than a smaller college town. Another clue we ignored.

We received the information from the university, and Andrew was registered and assigned a dorm room with a roommate. At Andrew's request, we had asked for a single room. Normally they want freshman to have a roommate, but Andrew was insistent on having a single room because of his problem with migraine headaches. He needs controlled lighting—a flash of light can set off a migraine. We wrote a letter to the university and explained his concern and this potential conflict if he had a roommate. They graciously accommodated his request and gave him a single room. I now believe there was another reason: he didn't want another guy in his room.

## Andrew finds love at the University of Minnesota

As we put the tape on rewind, there was yet another incident that was withheld from us. He was quite sick during the first semester of his freshman year. On top of the usual adjustments, his prolonged ill health interfered with his studies. That is not surprising as it happens to many students as they adjust from high school to college, be it stress, not eating the right food, or just learning a different venue. Whatever the reason, it complicated his concentration on his studies. He told us later that Jaysen, a boyfriend he met his freshman year, pulled him through that first semester. He is quite sure that if not for him, he may have had a short college career. We, of course, didn't know how vulnerable he was and didn't know about Jaysen. We are pleased to say that Jaysen and Andrew have been together ever since and are now living in Las Vegas.

I hope this gives you some insight into Andrew. We don't know if Brad's "mistakes" (reasons for us to suspect he was gay) drove Andrew deeper into the closet. We don't know if Andrew saw himself clearer because he recognized Brad was gay. But we do know that these brothers love each other very much and have helped each other along the way. That is all that counts with us. The rest really doesn't matter.

# Finally—An Explanation of "True"

*"Becky was the only friend he confided in regarding his 'true self.'"*

Andrew and his friend, Becky, had this annoying nickname of "True." They never called each by their first name, it was always True this and True that. When we asked about the nickname, there was never a response. It was a secret that only the two of them had, and they held it close to their chest.

As I recall our inquiries about True, I realize a clue was given. Another one of his friends asked one time why she couldn't be "True." The response was that Brad could be in the True club but she couldn't. That should have been a neon sign to us, but we weren't considering the option that Andrew was gay.

That Thanksgiving night, the explanation of True was finally revealed to us. Becky was the only friend he confided in regarding his "true self." She held that secret for him for one and a half years. She was a loyal friend to Andrew. We will always be grateful to her for giving him an avenue to discuss who he was with someone he could trust.

# Son Number Two **Comes Out: A Christmas Letter**

---

*"Paul and I know we were chosen*
*to have Brad and Andrew as our sons."*

---

We selected a different avenue for telling our family and friends about Andrew. After consulting with Andrew, we decided to write a letter and let everyone know at the same time. We've included the entire Christmas letter we sent to our family in 2001.

### 2001 Christmas Letter – A Special Edition

Paul and I are writing a special holiday letter to our families this year. This is not a usual Christmas letter that we have sent in the past. This year we have something to share with you that isn't the ordinary year-in-review news.

Several years ago Paul and I made our rounds to our family members to tell you that our son, Brad, was gay. We were blessed with support from our friends and our family. As you know, Brad and Chad made a lifetime commitment to one another and have made a wonderful life together. We consider Chad a member of our family and love him as our son.

This Thanksgiving our son, Andrew, told us that he is gay. Paul and I held him and told him how much we loved him.

There were no tears for who Andrew is as he has no control over his fate to love a man or a woman. The tears, as with

Brad, were for the pain he experienced as he dealt with this critical issue in his life without the help and support of his family. The tears were for the many people in this world who don't understand that our two boys have not made a choice about their sexuality—this is who they are. Who would make such a difficult life choice if they felt there were other options for an easier path in their life?

Paul and I know we were chosen to have Brad and Andrew as our sons. God has entrusted them to us knowing we will love them unconditionally and care for them in the way in which they deserve to be loved and supported.

I know that for some of our family, Brad's announcement caused much soul searching. For many of you Andrew's news will come as a surprise and the soul searching will begin again.

What we ask of all of you is to support our sons with your continued friendship and love. A priest was quoted as saying—"don't turn your back on them now—they need your love now more than anytime in their life." That is what we will do and what we hope you will do as well.

*We love you all,*
*—Hjordy and Paul*

# Parents Open the Closet Door:
# Telling family, friends, and relatives

---

*"You carefully select people
whom you feel you can trust."*

---

You start with people who love you, who love your children, and the friends you trust most in your life. It is an emotional experience every time you "come out" to others, and you carefully select people whom you feel you can trust with this information—especially in the beginning. The following short summaries include our friends who revealed their own stories. We found that we were not alone—we are one of many who have a story to tell.

## A friend's brother

Little did I know that one of my best friends has a gay brother. When I told her about Brad, she readily shared her brother's identify. I knew she would be open to the idea of having a gay family member, but I was surprised to hear about her brother. Why didn't she share this with me before my admission?

## A co-worker's brother

I couldn't tell my secretary the day after we found out about Brad, but within the week I sat down with her and recounted my week. She was very understanding and a good listener. Tears glistened in her eyes, and I quickly realized there was something else going on. Surprisingly, she shared with me that she had a gay brother. The tears were well-founded, as his news to his family was not accepted by all family members. She was struggling with trying to bring her family together by overcoming a homophobic reaction by her father.

## My college roommate's sister

You never know for sure what kind of a response you will receive from your friends and family. Our best friends from college hold many attachments to our life through our college years and after. My girlfriend and I had a double "blind" date on Valentine's Day in 1970. We both ended up marrying those two wonderful men. We nurture our relationship to this day. We both had two sons, and all four of the boys were swimmers. It was interesting how parallel our lives had become.

We wrote an e-mail to them as we didn't have any immediate plans to visit them. We thought it would give them some time to think about our news and wouldn't put them on the spot like it might have if we told them in person. We found that we used a variety of strategies depending on who we were telling.

We didn't hear from them for quite some time, so we wrote back. They were 100 percent supportive of us and of Brad. They said they had their own story to share but would wait until we saw them next time.

When we saw them a few months later, they told us that my girlfriend's sister was a lesbian. It was a well-kept secret from all but one other family member. Her sister was not confident telling her parents or some of her siblings. I felt bad for her and realized again that not all families have the support that our sons had. Another reason we feel that it is important to tell our story.

We are happy to report that my girlfriend's sister has told her mother and other siblings, met and "married" a nice young lady, and they are very happy. Her mom attended their ceremony and has kept an open mind about her daughter.

# Boyfriends Are **No** Different Than Girlfriends

*"Their relationship is everything that you see in a dating heterosexual couple."*

We have had several introductions to boyfriends over the last ten years. We anticipated each meeting with the usual parental concerns. Will we like him? Does he treat our son respectfully? Will he love our son as he deserves to be loved? Will they be financially stable? Will he be loyal?

Was it strange to meet a boyfriend instead of a girlfriend? We can't say it was. Their relationship is everything that you see in a dating heterosexual couple. We never discussed our disappointment in seeing our son with a man instead of a woman. Once we accepted our son's sexual preference of a male versus a female, we didn't look back.

Brad's first boyfriend that was introduced to us was a very interesting young man. You could get lost in his blue eyes, and he was full of fun. Even though the relationship was one of his first serious dating experiences, it only lasted a few months. They were both young and immature in the dating scene. We think, as with most early dating experiences, that he had a serious crush and there just wasn't enough substance and too few common interests to hold them together.

Brad's second serious relationship was Chad. There was an immediate bond between Chad, Paul, and me. He loved to talk politics, work, and wanted to know everything about Brad. Our time spent together was always full of fun, laughter, and lots of discussions. Their relationship lasted a little more than five years, and then they decided it wasn't working out. Just like a heterosexual relationship, this "divorce" was very sad and tragic for all of us. We loved Chad and still do. We are happy they both found happiness with someone else.

Brad's current partner is quite different from him. You know the old saying, opposites attract! He is an actor and very artistic, which are not necessarily Brad's strongest talents. Their different skills and attributes compliment each other. They both love to travel, like theater, enjoy movies, and love a clean house. They have a busy life because both of them are involved in many after-hour interests. Brad's "father-in-law and mother-in-law" are a wonderful support system to both of them. All four of the boys' "in-laws" recently helped with the Target booth during the PRIDE celebration in Minneapolis. They are there for them, and we appreciate that very much.

Andrew's first few boyfriends are unknown to us. He was dating without our knowledge, so we never had an opportunity for a reaction to his first two boyfriends. He met his partner, Jaysen, his freshman year of college in 2002. We were introduced to him at a Christmas party at Brad's house. My first reaction was, "Oh my goodness, he is tall." I didn't get an immediate feeling of Jaysen or their relationship. Over a few more meetings throughout the next year, I saw affection and true caring between them. As their love grew, there has never been a doubt in our mind that they love each other and are bound by that love in a long-term commitment. They love their families, their dog, their work, and their life in Vegas. Their life is like any heterosexual couple. Their household duties and financial management have been shared between them. They have hopes, dreams, and plans for the future. They have been together since 2002 and have beaten the odds of many married couples in the United States.

Don't be afraid of that first encounter with a boyfriend or girlfriend. I liken it to entering the swimming pool. It might be hard getting wet when you first go into the water, but it becomes comfortable and enjoyable once you are fully submerged and you become acclimated.

# Friends

> *"They continue to love, not judge, our family."*

When we think of friends, words such as *confidant* and *loyalty* come to mind. Friends are our neighbors, buddies, and girlfriends from high school, college, church, and work.

Our friends were supportive when we disclosed that Brad and Andrew were gay. They heard this announcement twice from us. We walked away from each announcement with a better understanding of what love of a person really means. We saw that our friends loved our boys and it didn't matter who or what the situation was. Both of us believed that this news was not to be silenced but instead rejoiced. As days, months, and years have passed, our friends are still present in all of our lives and continue to love, not judge, our family. They have never let us down.

# The Massage Therapist Discloses Her Suspicions

---

*"I believe I was meant to be in that place at that time."*

---

I was anxiously awaiting one of my favorite indulgences—a visit to my massage therapist. I was seated in the waiting area, and Kay, the massage therapist, was on the phone. I didn't want to listen to her personal conversation, but I couldn't help but hear her. From the tone and words, I gathered that her son was a very good student but that lately his grades were not what they would expect from him. Kay wanted to help in any way possible to work with the school and with her son to turn the downward trend to a positive direction.

When Kay hung up the phone, I commented that I hadn't meant to eavesdrop but had overheard her conversation. I said her son's problem was probably symptomatic of a bigger issue. She immediately responded with, "Yes, I think I know what is wrong. I believe my son is a homosexual." I was shocked that she so easily shared that with someone she didn't know very well. At that point she had no idea I had a gay son. She shared her clues and some unfortunate homophobic incidents that occurred in her son's school. Once on the massage table, the conversation continued. I told her that we had a gay son. That opened up an entire hour of conversation.

At the conclusion of our session, I felt that I had helped another parent with her questions and struggles. I believe I was meant to be in that place at that time. I sure didn't have all the answers, but I did have experience.

The story doesn't end there. Kay and I kept up with our boys and where they were and what they were doing over the next few years. One session, however, there was another turn in the road. I had previously told her when Andrew revealed that he was gay, so she knew that we had two gay boys. Much to my surprise, I now learned that we share the common factor of having two children who are homosexual. She told me about her suspicions regarding her daughter and the conversation that finally occurred when her daughter told her she was a lesbian.

I admire Kay a great deal. She has never wavered in her support of her two children. They have always known they are loved, and the fact that they are homosexuals has become a part of their "normal" life in their family. Kay graciously agreed to write something for this book. Don't miss her story. She is an amazing mom.

# A *Will & Grace* Story:
## Ursula and Jürg

---

*"We learned that relationships take many forms and fill different needs. Ursula taught us that there can be love between a woman and a gay man."*

---

We had the pleasure of hosting a foreign exchange student from Switzerland during Brad's junior year of high school. We promised her we would come to Switzerland when she found that special someone and decided to get married. Barbara and her family and friends had visited us since her exchange years, but we had never been to Switzerland. When she announced her engagement, we excitedly planned for our two-week trip. We couldn't wait to meet her fiancé, family, and friends we had heard so much about when Barbara lived with us.

Soon after we arrived, we were having a leisurely talk on their outdoor patio. Barbara's mother, Ursula, has been a good friend ever since our sponsorship year with her daughter. It was not unusual to have a conversation about personal matters. To our surprise, Ursula was in the midst of a separation from her husband. We didn't realize it had gone to that level. It was an unfortunate situation, especially at the joyful time of their daughter's marriage.

Ursula knew she must reveal the situation with her current husband as it wouldn't take us long to figure it out. What we didn't know was she had developed a loving friendship with another man—a man who was gay.

The warning flags went up immediately. Was she falling in love with a man who could not give her a full relationship? Was he taking advantage of her in any other way? Paul and I are very open-minded, but this caused some question marks. Other than the TV show, *Will and Grace*, this was a new one for us!

I watched Ursula as she told us about Jürg. Her eyes sparkled and her mouth was curved in an endless smile. We concluded immediately that he made her very happy. Once she started talking about Jürg, she couldn't stop. He obviously filled a void in her life.

We stayed with Jürg and Ursula at her lake home in Italy. It gave us a chance to talk with Jürg and see the two of them together. They were incredible. All we saw were loving comments, gestures, and a couple who had a lot of fun together.

During one of our evening meals, Jürg posed a question to us that we were not prepared to hear or to answer. He asked us if we were ready for Brad to have multiple partners throughout his life. We hadn't thought about that as Brad was in a committed relationship and we felt it would be forever. I guess Jürg's experience provided us with another possibility that we should have considered before. As it turned out, he was right.

In four years we returned to Switzerland to celebrate the birth of Barbara and Michael's twins. Ursula and Jürg are still together and happy. Their relationship has stood the test of time. We learned that relationships take many forms and fill different needs. Ursula taught us that there can be love between a woman and a gay man.

# Eleven Years Later:
## Has there been a change?

*"If the people who are supposed to love one another
the most can't accept family members for who they are,
what is our hope for those who don't have a reason to
dig in and explore their biases and homophobia?"*

We had a big family gathering at a resort with the majority of my husband's family. It was a huge undertaking, which I organized. Most of the family seemed grateful for the effort. The arrangements, food, and activities were designed to encourage fun and fellowship. At the end of the weekend there were requests for more gatherings like this. I was happy everyone had a good time but walked away quite disturbed and sad about some of the statements that were made by our nephews during the weekend. We really thought biases and homophobia were behind us, but we found out that was not the case.

Our oldest son is one of the top fitness instructors in Minneapolis. He is a trained professional fitness instructor, has been a fitness trainer of trainers, does special work with a large corporation's employees, has been asked to make a fitness video, and has full classes every time he teaches. He was excited to do a fitness walk with interested family members on two of the mornings during the weekend. We all gathered and went for a walk with exercises mixed in. All who went enjoyed the experience.

Later in the evening two of the cousins felt it was worth a quick laugh to make fun of this experience. It went something like this: "I told my wife that if she went on another one of those walks, I would divorce her." (As it was repeated to us, the innuendo was that he didn't want his wife participating in "gaylike" activities led by our son.) Of course it brought laughter from the others standing around him at that time.

The second comment was made during a volleyball game by another cousin who was mocking Brad's stretching exercises before and after the walk. "Now, let's stretch everyone," (laugh, laugh, laugh) he said as he mocked the way Brad did his stretching routine.

I am not sure why the two of them would go after the quick laugh at the expense of one of their cousins. The jokes did two things: the cousins embarrassed themselves by showing their lack of knowledge about fitness and Brad's status in the fitness world, and we realized they were unaware they were revealing their homophobia.

The third incident that was quite telling of how yet another cousin feels about our son was during a night of drinking. My son went to get him from a party next door, where he wasn't invited, and steered him back to our rental unit. He shrugged my son off with the following statement: "Leave me alone, you *faggot*." I guess people say what they mean when they are drunk. Obviously he hasn't grown in his understanding in the last ten years. This was the most hurtful incident of all. When I hear the word *faggot*, it feels hateful.

We love our nephews, but these incidents disappointed and saddened us. We have tried very hard to overlook many things over the years. What happened that summer was probably our biggest disappointment because we thought the cousins had come a lot further than that in the ten years since Brad's coming out. If the people who are supposed to love one another the most can't accept family members for who they are, what is our hope for those who don't have a reason to dig in and explore their biases and homophobia? The answer scares us.

# PART II

## REFLECTIONS FROM DAD

# A Touch on the Shoulder

---

*"You never know when that 'touch' is going to happen."*

---

On Easter day of 2008, I listened to a sermon by Reverend Schuller titled, "A Touch on the Shoulder." As usual, his message made me think and apply it to my personal life.

What if you were touched on the shoulder? How would you react to news such as

- ✔ I love you
- ✔ I'm dying
- ✔ I dropped Grandma's vase
- ✔ I lost my keys
- ✔ I'm getting a divorce
- ✔ I'm sick
- ✔ Could I marry your daughter?
- ✔ I'm not going to college
- ✔ I'm moving
- ✔ I'm gay

We've experienced many "touches" through the years. Our reactions covered an array of feelings. We always felt good that others thought our shoulders were "touchable."

The one touch that we weren't prepared for was, "I'm gay." When Brad touched our shoulder, he knew he was ready to share the news and felt we could handle it. I'm happy that he felt safe in touching our shoulder.

You never know when that "touch" is going to happen. We hope that our story, reflections, and advice will help you when someone taps your shoulder.

# Paul's Top Ten List

What would Dave Letterman's *Late Show* be like without the Top Ten? Viewers expect to be entertained by the issues of the day, week, or month. I don't always understand why a particular phrase is included on the list. I don't know if his list of the magical ten is ranked in order of importance. I do know that the audience rates this as a vital part of his show.

I have a Top Ten list for parents of a gay son or daughter. After much reflection, I consider these ten tips to be my best advice for a parent of a gay family member. Each of my Top Ten headings is followed by my reflections. I hope this list will allow you to think about your own situation. Who knows? Maybe this thinking might lead to a smile or laugh as you work through your own personal situation. But most importantly, I hope it impacts your life in a positive way.

# 10: Have an Open Mind

## So you asked

*"Your response is a definite indicator of where you have evolved with your inner self."*

As parents of two gay boys, you always have to be prepared for this question. What is the question? Through general daily conversations you will be asked how your children are doing. The questions will usually lead to *the* question: "What about a girlfriend/boyfriend?" This is your moment of TRUTH. You have seconds to answer the inquiry, which can cross into your safety zone. Your response is a definite indicator of where you have evolved with your inner self.

There is no right or wrong way of sharing this information. At first we thought this would be a dreaded question. We finally found that our only response was, "Our boys are gay." Those four words have become so natural for us now—that is the only answer we give today. Some of the responses or actions lead to some very interesting dialogue, but that will be discussed later. We are comfortable now, but our listeners don't always look or act comfortable about our response, which inspired my next selection on nonverbal language.

## A picture is worth a thousand words

*"The range of responses varies from
silence to a joyful acceptance."*

I once drew a picture for an English composition class in high school. The teacher accepted this shortcut to a writing assignment. I never realized that the thousand-word picture would come back later in my life. The picture that I refer to today is the response we get when we reveal our boys are gay. I have noticed so many different pictures develop; the range of responses varies from silence to a joyful acceptance. Body language says so much at this moment. I have seen faces turn red, tears in corners of eyes, looks of puzzlement, nods, hugs, and the list goes on. I have found over this time that people are initially in shock from your answer. This shock is usually followed by a short silence. Following this quiet moment is some form of a testimonial about their friend or family member who is a homosexual. The "picture" starts to take on a special look at this time. You are speaking the TRUTH, and they are sharing with you their reaction to this news that you shared with them. At this time you decide what to say. The picture, the experience, is on the canvas, and you are the artist. This is a special time to paint your thoughts and establish scenes for the next level of conversation. Remember that you are the artist and the picture needs time to be viewed.

## How did Dad really take the news?

*"How different our life would be if I hadn't
considered new possibilities."*

53

My oldest son, Brad, and I have memory gaps on his coming out day and the immediate time preceding that day. As Brad started reading the rough draft of this text, he expressed puzzlement over certain events. He feels like some things have been blocked out in his mind. I told him the same thing had happened to me. I try to think back to those emotional moments, and there is a loss of the time line for that day. My wife can remember in detail events that I can't. I listen to her and wonder if I was even there.

This memory loss does not worry me. We go back often to reflect and try to replay the script. As the four of us recall the seconds, minutes, and hours of that day, the pictures become less confusing.

I asked Brad if he remembered my immediate reactions to his news. I reminded him not to hold back any recollection of my initial response and later thoughts during that time.

Brad said I didn't get mad or rant and rave. He said there were many questions and concerns. Topics such as AIDS and celibacy were high on my list. I was concerned about the danger of diseases. Could or would he remain at home? What was in the future for him? Was Brad in harm's way?

On that "coming out" evening, we talked for about an hour or so. The next day brought me new questions and answers. I had gotten over the first hurdle. I remember my wife and I were confused, hurt, and very puzzled as we hugged and kissed Brad before departing to our bedroom. I remember that night's sleep was preempted by many tears. I am sure prayers were said and sleep finally settled in during the wee hours.

The next morning came before we knew it. Both of us had our jobs to get ready for. I remember when Brad came to the kitchen. He seemed like there was no loss of sleep on his part. In fact, he said he slept like a baby. I am sure the world was off his shoulders and he was ready to move on.

This was the beginning of a new chapter for us. We started that day with heavy hearts and weren't quite sure what to expect or where to turn next.

Did I have an open mind? I know my world has expanded since that fall day when Brad told us he was gay. I don't live in a black-and-white world anymore. How different our life would be if I hadn't considered new possibilities.

## Second gay son?

*"Once he told us, my mind was immediately open to a different vision of his future."*

The possibility of having a second gay son never entered my mind. Andrew was his own person, and we gave him many more freedoms than Brad. He never seemed to take advantage of this independence. He kept his studies up, excelled in sports, and was always on the move. The one thing Andrew didn't do was date often or have a steady girl. We just didn't think much of this because he was so busy. There was never a reference to him being gay. It is really amazing how Andrew kept this from us. He was a master at hiding it deeply. He probably learned from his brother what *not* to do. He hid safely in his closet.

I guess, in this case, my mind was closed to the possibility that Andrew was gay. I am not sure why I didn't consider that possibility, but once he told us, my mind was immediately open to a different vision of his future.

## Lectures gone astray

*"Little did we know that the girls were safe and sound with our boys!"*

As parents, many of us dread our son or daughter's dating years. Probably the parents that have girls fear this time period even more. There is so much out there that your children can be exposed to— where do you start with your advice and guidance?

All of us set guidelines for the dating process. You want to know the when, where, why of this new person in your child's life. You most likely walk the floors and stay up until they return home from the big date.

Well, we did the same thing with our boys. Little did we know that the girls were safe and sound with our boys! I think back and try to picture if Brad or Andrew had a smile on their face during the big lecture times. They were patient with us and allowed the nervous parents to express their concerns.

The good thing about the lectures back then was they were practical for any relationship. I am sure the advice was adapted to their dates later on.

We smile and laugh, as the boys do, over this parental concern time. I am lucky that the boys had a sense of humor about this as they could have construed my instructions about their manhood in a very different way. Should you make your parenting lectures generic? It is something we hadn't considered, but now you have something to think about!

## The sons-in-law

*"During this dating time we observed all the same highs and lows that parents experience with heterosexual relationships."*

Our daughter-in-law mind-set took a sharp turn during the coming out days of our sons. As you know, we experienced those events twice. As "rookies" in the gay community, we had much to learn or unlearn, or at least we thought so.

We went through the infant, terrible twos, off to school, adolescence, and young adult years surviving most days feeling successful. Now we were presented with a new challenge—or was it so new? We faced each one of those growing up years with no more knowledge than we had for the coming out era. The big difference during this time was our boys assuring us that they would guide us through this transition. We were in the habit of setting the standard, but now our sons would help us understand something they had far more experience with.

The beautiful part about this early transition was that we were able to see our sons express sincere love for another person. Yes, we were in the mind-set of a future "daughter-in-law," but this image was only changed by one word: *son*-in-law. Our boys could now express their true feelings in front of Mom and Dad. We saw how happy they were.

As parents we had all the same concerns that were there before knowing our boys were gay. We told the boys to be safe, take your time, and come home as often as you like. During this dating time we observed all the same highs and lows that parents experience with heterosexual relationships. Our boys prepared us for this, and we were ready. Our mind was open to a new paradigm.

# 9: Get Educated

## The View

> *"I am still impressed by the openness of the hosts and their respect of the various viewpoints."*

One of my favorite television programs is *The View*. I have been watching this since it first aired. My favorite part is the first twenty minutes. You never know what the topic or story will be or where it will lead on that day or days to follow.

We got a firsthand look at this show while visiting New York City. We were part of the audience for two shows on a special filming day. This visit only made our TV watching more of a daily ritual.

Since that time, Rosie came and went. We loved Star and miss her view. Rosie took the show to an elevated level. I loved her openness on all the topics. I especially appreciated her willingness to share gay topics with the world. Rosie spoke about issues and held nothing back. Her stories about Kelly and her family were warm, thoughtful, and caring. The other members of *The View* were supportive, and the feeling of acceptance came easily by the other *View* members.

Even though Rosie is gone, the format is still the same. The issues are as hot as ever, and you still feel engaged in the discussion. I am impressed by the openness of the hosts and their respect of the various viewpoints. Every day you have the potential to get educated on new topics with various viewpoints.

## Information is a powerful tool

---

*"Our biggest help has been our boys."*

---

We know some of the jargon. During the fifties and sixties, the whispered word was *queer*, which has now come back as an accepted term for people who are not heterosexual. The *gay* title seemed to spring up later in our life. The word *homosexual* was a common choice through the eighties, nineties, and is still considered the proper lay term today. I am sure a new descriptor is in the brew. I ask myself sometimes, is a term necessary? Our society likes to categorize and label people.

Until our middle to senior years of parenting, we were totally new to much of the gay life. For much of their pre- and post-adolescent years, our sons kept us in the dark. Then we found that a whole new world was going to be explored by our boys and us. All of a sudden we felt the need to get educated. Hjordy is an avid reader, so books immediately gave her insight. Obviously our boys coached us along as well. One show that introduced us to this jargon was *Will and Grace*. This show provided us a lighthearted view of our new challenge. That is where we were introduced to the expression *"fag hag."* Boy did that open another experience for us.

We constantly ask our sons what certain words, phrases, and actions stand for. As we watch *Will and Grace*, about one-third or more of the dialogue goes right over our head. We know we are "getting educated" because our laughs during the show have increased over the years.

The media, books, television, movies, and plays have helped us to understand more terms and jargon. Our biggest help, again, has been our boys. We talk often via the phone, e-mail, letters, and visits. They get us engaged in their daily living. We feel more and more connected as each day passes by. Communication is the key to getting educated. Show an interest in your son or daughter's world, and you will be a lifetime partner in their adventure.

To assist you in potentially awkward moments, I have prepared a list of current terminology we have adopted in our family. For example, what is the "correct" phrase or word that should be used for our son's friend? Is it *boyfriend*, is it his *significant other*, or perhaps his *partner*? Certainly this is a personal choice, so review the following list and adopt your own terminology.

**homophobic.** Prejudice against lesbian, gay, bisexual, and transgender people.

**gay.** Males who experience a sexual attraction toward other males.

**lesbian, lesbo.** Females who experience a sexual attraction toward other females.

**boyfriend.** A male partner in a non-marital romantic dating setting.

**partner.** Someone who is involved with your son or daughter in a primary relationship; sometimes referred to as a *life partner.*

**married.** Joined in matrimony.

**commitment ceremony.** Any ritual for honoring the union of lesbian or gay couples.

**lifestyle.** A way of living.

**queer.** A person who is not heterosexual.

## A safe place

> *"The physical or emotional damage that results from a bully can adversely affect a child."*

As a former educator and also a parent of two boys, I strived to have a safe place for my family and the children in my care at school. What do I mean by a safe place? That place would be where all could go and feel unrestricted by worries. Through their growing up years, those safe places were thought to be schools, parks, homes, and churches.

Much of my expertise centers around schools. How safe are they? On a rating scale, the schools would be average to slightly above average. For me, that is not good enough. Schools have to keep a better eye out for "bullies." The physical or emotional damage that results from a bully can adversely affect a child. Teachers and parents need to listen to their children when this red flag is waved. Often confessions of being bullied are dismissed as tattling. I know how scary this can be for children.

A safe place for all is an issue that needs to be addressed on an ongoing basis. Fear of bullies affects the child in their social, emotional, and educational progress. It could happen at recess, lunch, before and after school, or during the school day.

Parents need to go to their teacher and talk about the concerns that are expressed by their son or daughter. This place where your child spends much of their time—school—needs to be evaluated to make sure it's actually a "safe place."

We created a checklist for educators in the resource section of our book, part IV. Many of the suggestions for educators can be a benefit to parents. Be a partner in your child's education by keeping informed of policies and procedures that protect your child in the school setting.

# 8. Practice Tolerance

## The bashing

> *"We are both former teachers and have witnessed some of the worst bashing in our school hallways."*

Both my wife and I are very sensitive to the gay bashing that we have witnessed. We have felt very uncomfortable in many settings. Sometimes the bashing appears innocent and at other times it is out-and-out abuse. No matter what the setting is, it is time for it to stop. The bashing comes in the form of jokes to party talk and occurs everywhere, from sporting events to schools. We are both former teachers and have witnessed some of the worst bashing in our school hallways.

Children often repeat what they hear, so this problem might be deeper than the hallways. Yes, I am referring to the home. Children seem to be empowered by the phrase "That's gay." This expression leads to other forms of bashing as children mature. Most homes teach and expect tolerance toward others; parents should ensure their children practice tolerance everywhere. Our dream is to see a day when no one will be labeled and have hurtful words aimed at them. Yes, we strive for the perfect world! And yes, it will require educating the masses about a group of people who seem to be the open target for inappropriate remarks and actions.

## Lifestyle

---

*"Hopefully that tolerance will lead to acceptance—acceptance that being gay is not their lifestyle but instead it is their life."*

---

Lately we've heard friends, relatives, and the general public use the word *lifestyle* when referring to gays. I sense that the people using this term are still not sure if someone can *really* be gay. Part of me feels that they think there is a choice in being gay. Another part of me is confused with this way of thinking.

Most of our relatives and friends have known Brad and Andrew since they were little boys. They were informed of our sons' "coming out" periods within weeks after the announcement. Their use of this term, *lifestyle*, tells me that there is an uncertainty of who our boys really are in their eyes. I also hear the phrase *lifestyle choice* used about other people that they know are gay.

Many people think being gay is still a choice and not the essence of a person. Their thought process of being gay is that it's a lifestyle someone chooses. When *lifestyle* is applied to gays, my radar says people who use this term are holding prejudice against our sons and other families with homosexual children.

In our situation, our relatives and friends have come a long way since first hearing the news that Brad and Andrew are gay. The degree of acceptance varies from person to person and family to family. We hope someday that everyone will be on board. A good starting point is tolerance for their lifestyle, but hopefully that tolerance will lead to acceptance—acceptance that being gay is not their lifestyle but instead it is their *life*. Don't miss the special article on lifestyle by Virginia Wolf in part V.

# The rainbow connection

*"We love our hobby and are very happy that the rainbow connection is for everyone."*

My wife and I collect Wizard of Oz memorabilia. We started this hobby when my father passed away. Our family owned a few of the Oz books. When I was young, my Dad would read us these stories and make up many other tales involving the Oz characters. We all fell asleep many times for naps and bedtime with lions and tigers and bears jumping over the fence—oh my!

My wife and I inherited the Oz books and have added many more books along with a huge collection of Wizard of Oz memorabilia. As avid collectors, one of our favorite Oz and Judy Garland gathering places is Grand Rapids, Minnesota. Each year, this community celebrates a weekend in Judy Garland's honor.

Our yearly trip to this event has broadened our appreciation of Judy Garland, her talents, and her deep fan support. It continues to grow. It is an eclectic group of people where age, sex, and race do not matter for fans of Judy. It didn't matter because Judy accepted her fans for who they are. It has been written that gay men seem to have taken an interest in Judy Garland. In fact, some very dear friends of ours that attend these functions are gay couples.

I've included this passage as a connection. We love our hobby and are very happy that the rainbow connection is for everyone. If you ever come to Grand Rapids to the Judy Garland Festival, we would love to meet you and share our story with you.

# 7. Don't Burn Bridges

*"So often you get just one chance."*

My wife has always used this expression with the boys and me. As educators, we have had many situations arise where a bridge could have been burned during the communication process. I took great care in keeping the lines open with parents because one incident could cause a complete breakdown—a broken bridge. Taking time to listen with our ears and observing with our eyes has helped bridge most gaps from getting wider. So often you get just one chance. Bridges are connections. When connections are cracked or broken, they need to be fixed or someone can be hurt. Likewise, when the bridge is strong, we safely cross back and forth with few problems. This analogy is true with relationships. Make sure your communication bridge is strong so, when tested, your bridge doesn't collapse but rather becomes stronger. This is especially true during and following the coming out time.

Even though it took our boys many years to come out, I feel they knew the bridges that we connected over the years were solid. I am not sure if Hjordy and I knew that, by our general parenting, we were instilling trust with our boys. We didn't have a parenting strategy for letting our boys be who they are; this happened naturally without our interference. By practicing this philosophy, I feel that their confidence was enhanced when the time came to tell us. They were nervous yet confident that their story would be heard. Our bridge was strong. We had to take a dose of our own medicine in the first twenty-four hours; it was the moment that put our philosophy and practice in motion. I hope they continue this bridge building throughout their lives. I am so happy I have such a wise wife. She has helped me cross many bridges, and I know there are more to come.

# 6. Be a **Good Listener**

## Will you listen?

*"Listening opens doors that otherwise
may have stayed closed for a very long time."*

When we started writing this book, we said that the religious and political issues would not be our centerpiece. I will honor my wife's request on this and not speak to these issues in detail. My only comment at this time is regarding support. Your son or daughter will need you to be honest. Show your son or daughter you are willing to listen. If you are honest and are willing to listen, a major hurdle will have been overcome. Listening opens doors that otherwise may have stayed closed for a very long time.

Brad was the model in how he handled himself that fall evening in our family room. He, and then his brother, continues to be a model. They were good listeners when we had questions; we were good listeners when we received their responses.

We were also lucky that they let us go through our "mourning process." They allowed us to feel sad, ask questions, and learn before we embraced the updated vision of their futures. After all, they lived with this all their life; it was brand new to us.

## Grandpa knew

*"I really have to applaud my Dad for
being up-front with his concern."*

I can remember one day when my father and I had a discussion about Brad. I can't recall what we were doing at the time, but it was most likely playing cribbage, horseshoes, or watching a sporting event. Dad came right out and asked if Brad might be gay. For the moment I was thrown back by his question; it was so out of the blue. Dad said he noticed things about Brad that seemed different than other boys. He asked why Brad never talked about a steady girlfriend and also asked if he dated girls. He noticed how Brad avoided some of the "guy things" that the other nephews were involved in. He brought up conversations he had with Brad about general topics. Dad was curious and needed to share his thoughts with me.

I listened but was very uncomfortable inside. After he was finished with his questions, I responded. I think at the time I told Dad that his idea was impossible. I informed Dad that Brad did date and had girlfriends. Brad was always a gentleman and didn't do some of the typical teenage and young adult boy things.

When I think back to this event, I really have to applaud my Dad for being up-front with his concern. Little did I know that he was right. He was the only family member who spoke his mind to us. Maybe he was the elected spokesperson for other family members. As we found out later, many people suspected Brad was gay but never said anything to us.

Yes, I listened to my dad, but did I really hear him? I may have been too busy defending Brad's heterosexuality to really listen. If I had, what might have been different in how and when Brad came out? I can only guess.

# 5. Be Nonjudgmental

## Ten fingers and toes

---

*"We gave thanks for the obvious and cherished the unknown."*

---

I remember when both of our boys were born. We wanted to wait until birth before knowing the sex of our babies. As with all parents, we wanted a healthy newborn. The arrival showcased the usual examination of sex, hair, voice, ten fingers, and ten toes.

We were both overwhelmed by the births of our babies. Each boy had their unique way of entering the world. Our dreams, plans, and thoughts were lost in the moment during their arrival. All we could do was look at their beautiful bodies and thank God for the opportunity to be parents.

Our sons needed us to start our parenting. It was our job to provide a safe environment and create opportunities for them to develop and grow.

We saw their obvious features at birth, and now it was time for them to discover their new world. We gave thanks for the obvious and cherished the unknown. We probably had the purest heart those first few months. There were no judgments of what was wrong with our son. It was only joy of this beautiful child. Did we become more judgmental as time went on? Probably. Our advice to you as we look back is to follow your child's lead rather than to guide your children in the direction you want him or her to go. We did a little of both. We were lucky that there wasn't an imbalance that swayed our boys into something they didn't want to do or become.

## What went wrong

*"God knew you before you were born; no one is a mistake."*

*(Desmond Tutu)*

My answer is nothing went wrong. Brad and Andrew were conceived and born into life as the human beings they are today. This is our firm belief. They are children of God, and it is as simple as that. My wife and I experienced so many great moments with our boys during their formative years. Choices and opportunities flourished during this time at the Wagner household. We often look back and end up smiling over those precious moments. We could call this a before-and-after period in their lives. Sometimes we think of it as chapter 1 and chapter 2.

There are some who believe that our boys made a choice or that we should send them to counseling so they can become "normal." We say that you should accept them for who they are. Very simple.

## My Little Pony

*"If I could replay that scene with Brad, I would be combing the pony's hair with him."*

This book was not written overnight. It contains memories that date back to the early 1960s. This story happened around 1982. As a child, Brad had many toys and books that were age appropriate. His favorite toy at the tender age of five was My Little Pony. This character was the size of a hand. The unique feature was the pony's mane. The hair was longer than the animal itself. Brad loved to comb the horse's hair.

Back then I was concerned about his attachment to the horse. His constant combing of the mane became an issue for me. I thought that maybe this was more of a girl toy and Brad should be spending his time with other toys, such as GI Joe. I can remember hiding the horse only to see that he would find it.

The reason I am sharing this story is that a situation like this appeared on *The View* during the month of May 2008. The ladies were talking about proper toys for children. Sherri mentioned that she removed a doll from her son and replaced it with a truck. She wanted him to play with appropriate boy things.

I listened to the dialogue and thought of My Little Pony. If I could replay that scene with Brad, I would be combing the pony's hair with him. What result did my action have on Brad? I don't know for sure. I do feel I confused him by making judgments about his toys. I guess kids somehow survive their parent's mistakes.

# 4. Pray

*"My prayer background helped me during my childhood and adolescence, and has continued to be a primary occurrence for me each day."*

I remember my grandmother saying the rosary. She always carried a rosary with her. You could see the beads moving through her hands. As a child, I would ask her what she was praying for. She always had a list. Grandma was a worrywart, so if anything was in need of attention, she addressed that issue with her rosary and prayer.

Many years have gone by since my grandmother passed away. I don't know why, but I have started saying the rosary again. My fingers are the beads, and I find myself saying the rosary in the strangest places. My prayer background helped me during my childhood and adolescence, and has continued to be a primary occurrence for me each day.

The boys have assured me that they pray on a regular basis. Both Brad and Andrew find time to say a prayer some time during the day. This reflection of thought could occur at any time. It might happen while driving to and from work. Based on traffic in Vegas and Minneapolis, I think I would pray the entire time! No matter where or when the moment happens, they find time to reflect.

Hjordy's grandma, mom, and dad have always been devoted to the power of prayer. This was instilled in their family as it was in mine. One of the most memorable quotes from Hjordy's mom is, "Whenever the burden becomes too heavy, I hand it over to the Lord."

One of our first concerns was the view of the church regarding homosexuals. Since then we have learned that our connection to God through prayer is what has given us strength.

The view of the church is an important issue for many people when they find out they are a homosexual or they have a child who is a homosexual. We were no exception. If this is a concern to you, we suggest you find your answers through prayer. Whatever your affiliation, we wish you the best of luck in understanding this issue in the heart of God.

# 3. Show Your Support on Issues

## A friendly place to live

*"The big-city life offered many opportunities to find friends, family, and loved ones."*

One of our biggest concerns after our boys told us they were gay was the location they would pick for a place to live. We know each son loved their hometown, but a move was in the plan. Both boys chose their first "out of the nest" home in the Twin Cities area. Brad's choice centered around a place to be gainfully employed and accepted. Andrew's choice was a college education at the University of Minnesota. Having a child leave home is very hard for parents. At first we were nervous about the thought of a big city, but we found that the Twin Cities was not as big and scary as we perceived it to be. We showed our support of Brad's decision. He knew what he needed at that time.

Brad first introduced us to the fast-paced hustle and bustle of Minneapolis. Later, Andrew got us accustomed to big-city college life. As these two places became part of their daily routine, we grew less anxious. The big-city life offered many opportunities to find friends, family, and loved ones. As a parent, I would highly recommend the Twin Cities as a place to live for homosexuals of any age. The vast diversity in this community is seen each time we visit the area.

Brad is making Minneapolis his home. His job and other talents have fit into this community in so many positive ways. Andrew has moved to the warmer climate of Las Vegas. He calls this the land of opportunity. What we love about Vegas are all the things beyond the Strip. Andrew has tamed this big city and is making it his home.

## The network

> "*We are proud to see how he has bonded*
> *with such a diverse group of people.*"

Hjordy and I have attended many of Brad's social functions. First of all, we are overjoyed in being asked to be a guest at these special events. The events range from A to Z on the social calendars. Usually the gatherings have a mix of guests. Often we are the senior members of the group.

We are always welcomed by all. We are proud to see how he has bonded with such a diverse group of people. We feel a special connection with his friends. Brad and his partner always tell us how proud they are that we take an interest in their friends. One of our fears was a possible isolation of friends for our boys. That fear has been put to rest. We have witnessed a blend of friends and a strong support group that will always be there.

## First level of support

> "*I am not sure if these walls will come down*
> *or not, but I pray that they do.*"

One question that we thought of during the coming out time of our boys was their support group. We knew their immediate friends. That support group was already in place, but what would a new environment bring to them? It seemed to be an easy transition due to their personalities. Their openness drew people their way. The support from friends continued to grow.

Another support group was and still is on our minds. How would the cousins accept this news about the boys? I think the verdict is still out. At times I have witnessed a reservation on their acceptance of the boys. As parents you see, feel, and sense things. The cousin support has puzzled me over this period of time. I am not sure what it is, but I have some thoughts. I think some of the nieces and nephews are still confused. I know they love our boys, but they still hold questions about the boys' sexuality. I sense a protective shield has been put in place. These barriers have blocked the closeness that I know could develop. I am not sure if these walls will come down or not, but I pray that they do. I know that the boys love their cousins and need them. Hopefully time will break down any reservations that might still exist.

Of all the selections I have written, this is the most difficult one to express from my point of view. As parents, we have always tried to provide our boys with chances to interact with their cousins. I missed this interaction during my growing up years. We always strived to make sure Brad and Andrew knew their cousins. The closeness varied from person to person, but the opportunity for relationships was provided. Hopefully we will be here for many more years. When our time comes to leave this world, our wish is that the closeness will still be there for them through extended family. Who knows what form of support will be needed by others within our group? Now *that* is an interesting question, in that gay relatives are on both sides of the family.

How is the ongoing acceptance by the aunts and uncles? Again, I think this varies from person to person. Both Hjordy and I have families with deep roots, though we all share the highs and lows of a typical family clan. Time is set aside each year for family gatherings involving all members of our immediate brother/sisterhood. That piece was always in place and still is to this day. The siblings demand that we get together on a yearly outing. They know the importance of this bonding. Our boys love their aunts, uncles, and cousins very much.

Each aunt and uncle has had a unique way of sharing their feeling about the boys. I will not get into details, but I will say that our sons have honored each response that was given to them. They knew each person would have to process this news in his or her own way. We have been very proud of the boys and their openness to answer all questions. We are also proud of their patience as their friends and relatives grow in their understanding of their world.

## I do, and so much more!

*"Commitment is commitment no matter if the union of two people is by marriage or by the promise of fidelity to each other."*

In the gay and straight world, commitment should be the essence of any relationship. The life span of today's marriages is very scary. You hear numbers of 40–60 percent divorce rate. I don't know what the stats are for a gay/lesbian commitment. I can only guess that the numbers are about the same if not higher.

Commitment is commitment no matter if the union of two people is by marriage or by the promise of fidelity to each other. As parents, we expect this vow to be the same for all parties. We believe our boys feel the same way. Your expectations for your son or daughter should be that they are in it for the long haul. We believe a union is a union. It takes both to make it work. Putting the other person first is a great place to start.

As parents you need to commit to your son or daughter's relationship. You also now have a son-in-law or daughter-in-law that will need you in many ways. By giving of yourself and showing a sincere involvement, you will have provided a support system second to none.

# 2. Put Yourself in Their Shoes

*"I could see that the shoes filled by these people were much more diverse than what I imagined."*

Would you like to walk in their shoes? I have considered this question often throughout my life. As a youngster, I had dreams of being a professional football, basketball, baseball—you name it—player. I always thought, "If only I could be like *that* famous player." During my time that would have been Hank Aaron, Jim Taylor, Paul Hornung, Harmon Killebrew, Jerry Lucas, and many more. As a young person, I could only see the glitz and glamour of their stardom as a professional athlete. Those desires never came true for me, but it was fun dreaming. As I matured, those same dreams where there, but different role models came into the picture. During these formative years, I would wonder what the shoes of other individuals would feel and look like. With maturity comes reality. I could see that the shoes filled by these people were much more diverse than what I imagined.

As I write down my thoughts, I think of how the shoes of a homosexual fit. My wife and I can walk down any street holding hands. I can put my arm around her at a movie theater. We can kiss in any public place. The signs of affection between us are a form of love accepted by almost anyone in our society.

It saddens me when I think of my boys. The rules are just the opposite for them. If homosexuals are bold enough to show their affection in public, people stare, scorn them, use abusive language, and at its worse, physically respond. It is almost like the old E. F. Hutton commercial where everyone stops to listen and look.

Walk in their shoes? I have no idea what it is like. Our boys won't let me get bothered by it, but deep down I really do know, and it pains me. I hope we think more and more about those shoes. It would be nice if one size would fit all.

# 1. Look to the Future

## Fear not

---

*"You must transform your parental leadership role into a consulting, supportive network for your children."*

---

A respected television evangelist recently quoted that "fear not" is written in the Bible over three hundred times. How you interpret these words is between you and your God. Each of us will encounter times in our lives when we experience tough times. These moments could come and go. Sometimes they will hang on. Whatever the situation might be, we will have to deal with it. And we are not alone during these times.

As parents, we fear for our children. We know at a certain time that the younger ones must leave the nest. When this time arrives, you hope that you have provided the proper guidance. You must transform your parental leadership role into a consulting, supportive network for your children.

Fearing that our children were gay didn't enter our mind. We feared the everyday problems that our boys would face as they were on their own. Would they make the right decisions? Could they maintain a budget? Were they eating properly? Were they choosing good friends?

Being gay was never on our list. When we found out that they were gay, our fears overwhelmed us at first. We thought about situations that they would encounter that we had not prepared them for. But what we did not realize was that our boys were already prepared. They built on all the things we taught them and adapted them to their

This was our wedding day with our special grandmas. They both provided us with good values. Paul's grandma is mentioned in his chapter "Pray."

During a family vacation we had a Wild West photo taken of our family. Who knew that day what was ahead in our lives!

Unconditional love was tested when Hjordy's mom and dad found out their grandsons were gay. They got an A+ on that test.

Grandpa Orv, Paul's dad, suspected Brad was gay.
He died before his forecast was confirmed.

Chad and Brad had a touching commitment ceremony in Kauai. The sun slowly set just as the ceremony ended.

The commitment ceremony was followed by a delicious dinner on the beach. It was a memorable night that we didn't want to end.

Becky demonstrated her friendship and loyalty to Andrew when she held his secret that he was gay for more than a year.

Jill was a neighbor and friend of both boys. She was rocked by Brad's news and told him he was just confused! She continues to be a friend to both Brad and Andrew.

Ursula and Jürg, our special friends from Switzerland, have a special love that has withstood the test of time.

Andrew and Brad were talented athletes in high school. Both of them excelled in tennis and swimming. This photo was taken at a swim meet.

**Reprinted with permission from Julie Gilbert, Best Buy Senior Vice-President**

Brad is an experienced fitness instructor. This is a special event that he choreographed for the Best Buy WoLF employees.

**Reprinted with permission from *Instinct* magazine with
photo credit to Joe Schmelzer**

Andrew did some modeling that led him to this front cover
photo and article for *Instinct* magazine.

**Reprinted with permission from *Lavender* magazine with photo credit to Armour Photography**

Brad is seen faintly in the background of the front cover of *Lavender* magazine, a local gay magazine.

Andrew and Jaysen recently took a vacation in Maui. They have been together since 2001 and have made their home in Las Vegas.

Our family loved visiting Disney World. That tradition continues with Jaysen and Andrew as they enjoy their time at Disneyland.

Nathan and Brad enjoy the social opportunities in Minneapolis. There are numerous choices of things to do and places to eat.

new situation. They had developed support groups. They were okay. Once we realized this, we were less fearful. We looked beyond the fear and saw the happiness in their eyes. Nothing has changed as far as parental caring goes. We will still have our fears, but those fears are offset by the confidence that we have in our sons.

## 1 + 1 = 2 or 2 + 2 = 4

*"Each son has a loved one, so our two gay sons equal four gay sons."*

What does math have to do with our two sons? Well, the answer is simple. Each son has a loved one, so our two gay sons equal four gay sons.

Like the old saying...the more the merrier. We have thoroughly enjoyed our extended family. Our boys have included us in many of their functions. We are always welcomed guests in their homes. They are very good in attending family activities and gatherings.

Our boys and their partners ensure our life is never boring. We look forward to every visit, whether it occurs at our home or at their residence.

So, if you study the numbers, you can easily see that one becomes two, and two equals four. Who ever thought that math could be so rewarding? What will our future be with our four sons? We don't know for sure, but so far it has been adventure we want to watch from center stage.

## Our family tree

*"If the family tree stops with our boys, that is what is meant to be."*

What will our family tree look like? Will it stop where it is now? Is there a chance that a grandchild is in the future plans? Are Paul and Hjordy sad that the Wagner/Christison name will not have another chapter? Are our boys concerned about our branch of the tree ceasing to grow? Will there be an adoption or a surrogate mother?

Our only answer to the above questions is that we don't know. If the family tree stops with our boys, that is what is meant to be. The last thing we would want is for Brad or Andrew to think that this family branch needs an extension for Mom or Dad. We are very blessed to be parents. The boys are both miracles because we were told that children would be unlikely for us.

We never sit around and dream of grandchildren. Our main concern is for the well-being of our boys. We know each of our sons has thought of an extended family. We know this is for them to decide, and we will not influence any decision either way. We feel totally fulfilled with Brad, Andrew, and their partners. The family tree is firmly rooted with our boys.

# Why Write This Book?

The first response we heard when we asked, "Why write this book?" was, "You have to." This answer came from both of our boys. What was unique about the answer was that they were not asked at the same time. Brad was in Minneapolis and Andrew was in Las Vegas. We talked to each boy separately, but the same response was given to our question.

Another reason to write this book was our need to share our experience with others who could benefit. Both boys said this might not be as easy as we thought. They were exactly right. We wanted to share all of our feelings.

We want others to know that you can make it through this time. There are many ways to gain strength and courage as you process this new chapter in your child's life. We also want friends, relatives, and all the readers to know that we are here as a comforting ear.

As we were putting the final touches on the book, we had an experience that verified, once again, the importance of sharing our story, our journey.

One of Brad's friends called him while he was visiting us in Las Vegas. We were watching TV, and Brad's phone rang; he immediately went to another room. I knew it was something important as Brad normally didn't miss a moment of the show we were watching.

Brad told me later who called and shared with us that she was emotional about her brother, who had just come out to her. We both looked at each other and said, "We need to send her Hjordy's first chapter. We immediately e-mailed it to her so that she had something to reference, something to help her know that she is not alone and that her feelings are natural and normal. This was a final validation to us that we need to share our story, that our story has meaning for others.

In the next few weeks after that, we received other signs: a horoscope in both of our astrological signs that pointed to completing this book, a presentation talking about reaching others who are "outside of the circle," and from Janet, our former pastor, who assured us that our message is greatly needed in the hands of many people.

# PART III

## BRAD, ANDREW, AND GRANDMA SAY A FEW WORDS

# Over the Rainbow

*"My parents fostered a foundational value in me that is still present today: treat others like you would want to be treated."*

As you have read in previous chapters, my parents are active Wizard of Oz collectors. I felt this was an appropriate title for my chapter as it involves a symbol of the spirit, nature, and the beloved movie that taught me that dreams really do come true.

Those dreams, however, did not become a reality until later in my life. Sometimes there is unfamiliar weather and even storms that one must experience and live through before the clouds separate, the sun shines, and the beautiful symbol of light appears.

Have you ever looked at a couple or two people in love and wondered, will this ever happen to me? I remember many years thinking that I would never have this because I had not had the opportunity for love—not the kind of love that's real or authentic for me, anyway.

Being gay was scary for so long in my life. I didn't want to think about the possibility of being gay, as thinking about it meant that some sort of acknowledgment might surface, and I was not ready to face that so early on in my life.

As a parent, you might be asking: when do you know, how do you know, and why didn't you tell me earlier? Although everyone's story is different, I think there is a common word in the acceptance process for everyone, and that's "love."

To explore these questions, I will take you back a few years.

When I was approximately ten, I started to understand and realize that I was very sensitive to harsh words, discriminating words from others especially. These words were rarely said to me, but I was aware of the words as others were being picked on or teased at school. I have always had a radar for this type of bullying from others.

My parents fostered a foundational value in me that is still present today: treat others like you would want to be treated. This way of living is my golden rule. Notice how this statement doesn't have any "buts" or exclusions. It's simple, it's to the point, and it's real. The question is—do we do this?

As my friends today will tell you, one of my favorite words is "authenticity." Being authentic was not a part of my life for many years, as I was in a bubble consumed by my own fear: the fear of being accepted, the fear of acting a certain way, and the fear of letting my truth out. It was very lonely at times.

As I was going through the teen years, I knew that I felt an attraction toward other guys, but I didn't really understand these feelings. At times I felt as though there wasn't anyone like me. Living in Eau Claire, Wisconsin, you really didn't hear the word *gay* or *lesbian* or *homosexual* all that often.

One day sticks out more than the rest for me as I look back on my process of acceptance. It was a summer day, and we were on vacation from school. I was watching some morning television, and a preview for Donahue came on and the topic was "Growing Up Gay." I remember getting nervous and excited about this as there were rarely television programs about this when I was thirteen. This was 1990.

I had fifteen minutes before the show, so I told my dad that I was going downstairs, as that was sort of my place for privacy and relaxation. I put on the channel but sat close to the television just in case Dad came downstairs; I needed to be able to change the channel quickly to avoid suspicion.

Watching Donahue that day was an eye-opener for me. He had on gay people that were "normal." I don't like using this term, but at the time, that is what I felt. At that time in my life, I felt abnormal, like my thoughts were not making sense and that something was wrong with me. While I was watching that show, I felt as if I were watching a show that reflected my feelings and my thought process. I remember that moment vividly. I was excited after that show.

The next three years or so went by as they would for any normal teenager: sports, girlfriends, time with friends, family, etc. I wasn't ready to start talking about my feelings of possibly being gay; I didn't even explore it much in my head until I was sixteen.

Somewhere in my sixteenth year we went to see my grandma and grandpa. We stayed at their house with my parents. Andrew and I decided to play a game with some of my other little cousins: hide and seek. It might seem that I was a little too old for hide and seek, but my cousins were younger and we were all having fun.

During the countdown, I went in my grandparents' bedroom closet to hide, and Andrew followed me. After arguing with Andrew that he had to find his own spot, I pulled him into the closet to hide, as I knew they were already looking for us by then.

Andrew wouldn't stop talking, and then I heard a door shut. I knew it was from another room. I told Andrew to go and find another spot. During the commotion, a stack of magazines fell from the top of the closet. I quickly picked them up and found that they were "naughty" magazines. Andrew, of course, was inquiring about them, wondering what they were, and wanted to see them. I quickly put them back and we continued the game.

Later that night while my parents and grandparents were sitting on the porch, I went back to the room to see one of the magazines. I was curious. I remember pulling one of the magazines out and thinking to myself, "Wow!" I remember also that I was drawn more to the men in the photographs rather than the woman; this made me very anxious but excited at the same time. I took that magazine and kept it. This began the exploration stage of my sexuality.

About two years later I remember seeing information about AOL, the Internet service. My parents had a computer, but they didn't use it on a regular basis. I decided to sign up and start using the service.

I noticed one day that there were chat rooms in AOL. I decided to check them out. There were all sorts of chat rooms on every subject. While looking around, I noticed that there were chat rooms for the gay and lesbian population. I went in the chat room feeling very excited and nervous. There was a specific chat room labeled "Men 4 Men, Minneapolis." I went in. This was my first time seeing interactions with gay people. It was enlightening but also scary as a lot of the chatter was about sex. I wasn't as interested in that, more interested in talking to someone my age—about anything, really.

I eventually did start chatting with someone. His name was Matt. Matt was a competitive swimmer from southern Wisconsin, as I was. We hit it off in conversation quickly. He seemed like a nice guy, so we continued talking for hours online. This turned into a nightly occurrence for me; I really enjoyed talking to Matt.

During this time, my brother was always around wondering what I was doing. He was inquisitive and always in my business! My little brother was also very resourceful. One day, he got into my AOL account.

At the time, I was at the Athletic Club teaching a fitness class. He got into my account and found the conversations that I was having, along with other mail that I received—junk and spam mail, mostly. Andrew got confused and nervous by what he read and viewed. He told my parents, and when I got home, I had a lot of questions come my way.

I was somehow able to wiggle my way out of that situation. I think my parents weren't ready to fully face the fact that I was gay yet, and neither could I at the time. As I look back, I do feel that it was a stepping-stone to my future.

Matt and I eventually met about six months later; he is the first person that I ever met who was gay, and I will never forget that. He later moved to Minneapolis to attend school and we lost touch.

As you have heard from my parents, my coming out story went well. I know my parents were in shock in those early moments of learning I was gay, but I also knew that they loved me unconditionally.

It's hard to put into words the lessons, love, understanding, and teaching that my parents gave me as a child, but it has formed me into who I am today: a happy and secure person.

The message that I really want to convey to other parents is to understand that, from the view of a child, you are the ones that we look up to most in life. You give us clues, guidance, and values. I know so many gay people who have had a hard coming-out process, and my heart goes out to them. When there is a negative reaction from parents about their gay child, it's never about the child's confidence of who they are; it's about the parent's own fears. As a child, I have to have patience and remember what my fears of coming out felt like, as my parents have to go through their own coming-out process, and that takes time.

Once your family is able to make it through the rain and passed the initial storms that may surface, the light will appear and the clouds will separate and the dream of happiness will come true.

*—Brad*

# Family Bonds
## Triumph Over Everything

*"No matter what happened in my life, I
knew my parents loved me unconditionally."*

I knew I was attracted to the same sex by the time I entered kin-dergarten. I knew I didn't want to be with a girl. They were friends only—good friends, but only friends. In fact, I never dreamed about females or was attracted to girls in magazines as I observed other boys were.

A lot of girls wanted to date me. I was like a moving target in middle and high school. I moved in and out of a lot of different groups. Because of my personality, I never felt like I fit in any clique. I had friends of both sexes. Up until my senior year, I didn't think of dating men because I was concerned with grades and sports. Because of peer pressure, I did date for a couple of weeks when I was in ninth grade. That decision wasn't really mine but was driven by my friends. It was my friends saying "This is who you are seeing." She was a very nice girl, but we really never went on a date. I think she knew I wasn't into her emotionally or physically. In fact, I never kissed her, or any girl. I remember asking my mom, "Should I date or not date?" I didn't consider starting "dating" because of my parents; I wanted to get some of my friends off my back. I didn't want people to know my sexuality in middle or high school. If anyone asked me about dating, at least I could say I dated.

I felt more comfortable having female friends. I protected myself a little from males because I didn't want them to suspect or feel uncomfortable around me. Some may ask, what about my attraction to men in sports such as swimming and tennis? They were my peers, and it wasn't the time or place to even think about attraction—sports were sports.

During my junior year in high school, I told one of my trusted friends that I was gay. She held my secret for over a year. It was nice to be able to talk with at least one person about my feelings. After I told some of my other close friends my freshman year of college, one of my best friends was told by her grandma that she shouldn't be friends with me because I was gay. In the beginning, that friend felt that I made a choice to be gay. She has since changed her personal belief, and her grandma has accepted that we are friends.

I remember the night Brad told my parents he was gay. For me, it was a little bit different than Brad. At that time I knew that I was attracted to the same sex. Prior to that evening, I felt awkward for Brad. I knew he was living a lie and he was attracted to men as well. I knew when he was dating Katie that it was only friendship. I knew the truth. I tried to point out important clues to my parents. Even though I knew it was not my time to tell anyone, I was concerned for him.

When he finally did come out, I felt happy for him. I thought Brad could not be who he was until then. I always felt I was who I was, but with Brad it was different. Once he told my parents, he stepped through the door and became a different person.

My mom has asked me about my comment that memorable evening about having more kids to make up for Brad. I told my mom I would have kids, but I didn't say it would be with a female! That comment really gets to her to this day.

I used to go to Menomonie, a neighboring town, where I met some other people like me. I went to dance and to meet new people. It was about talking and hearing their stories. A few times I went to the cities to dance clubs. I did date two guys in the cities. I learned what it was like to be in a relationship—later than most young people. I really didn't know how to do it—I was back at the twelve- and thirteen-year-old stage wondering how to date. I was infatuated with them. I learned very quickly that I had to put up a wall with these two men because they were much more advanced than I was, and I didn't want that.

Jaysen came into my life my freshman year of college. We met online and then in person at the gym where I worked at the time. My first impression of him was he was good-looking and someone I would like to get to know more. We talked, went to movies, out to eat—the usual things. One thing led to another, and we have now been together seven years.

After meeting Jaysen, I knew it was time to tell my family. I waited until I was eighteen to tell my family because I really did not have a reason to tell them before that. My first real relationship happened at that time, and I knew bringing a guy to a family get-together would raise a couple eyebrows. Why didn't I tell them before? I really did not have a reason to tell my family before then because I was living my life like every other person. I woke up the same way, socialized the same way, and ate the same way every other human being did. I felt normal. If I did not have the support I did growing up, telling my parents I was dating a male would have probably been difficult. Because of the love of my family, it felt natural. Because of the love both of my parents gave to me, it wasn't such a hard thing to do.

As I reflect on my life so far, I realize how thankful I am for having such an amazing family. In my growing up years, my parents and brother let me know that no matter what I wanted to do in life, I could do it. My determination to achieve in academics and sports were in the forefront of my mind throughout middle and high school. Whatever bar I set in my mind, I knew it could be obtained because of my strong family bond. If I ever had doubt in my mind about achieving my dreams, I could always rely on my family for encouragement and support.

If I could give one message to parents out there, it would be to raise your children with all the love and support you can give. Because my parents made me feel that no matter what happened in my life they would love me, I felt at ease with sharing anything with them. My mom once told me that no matter what I did, she would love me unconditionally. She told me this long before I told her about my sexuality. Even though my dad didn't say that out loud, I knew he felt the same way. That stuck with me throughout my life, and I knew that no matter what happened in my life, I would be loved. Whether it was about my sexuality or anything else, I knew my parents would understand, and that was very comforting.

*—Andrew*

Suggestions for parents:

1. Let your child be who they are. Once you start telling kids how to be and who to be, it may result in rebellious behavior. In the case of a gay son, it probably forces kids deeper underground. Attraction to males is only one piece of your child.

2. Guide your child but don't force your child or pigeonhole your child into your interests. I was allowed to pursue my interests without interference from my parents. They supported my choices in sports and friends.

3. Show your love through your words and actions. If your child feels that love, anything seems possible.

# Being a Grandparent
# Is a Great Experience

---

*"It never crossed my mind to treat
them any different or love them any less."*

---

Holding a grandchild in your arms and rocking them brings out the love one has in one's heart. Before long, the little ones have grown enough to put their little arms around you and say they love you. That is the way it was with Brad and Andrew. Because they lived sixty-five miles away from us, we didn't get to see them as much as we liked. That was probably good because we would have spoiled them.

They were good boys growing up. Both of them are handsome and smart as a whip. I always kidded them that they got their smarts from their grandma—meaning me. They never believed me.

During Brad's high school days, I asked him several times about who he was dating. When he did take a girl out, he told me about it. None of them lasted very long. Andrew, on the other hand, had lots of girls who were friends. They would call him even before breakfast. To me, it looked like they were very normal boys.

That is why it was such a shock when I learned that Brad was gay. It knocked me for a loop. I struggled with it for a long time. I cried at times because I didn't and still don't understand why this had to be. My husband and I prayed about it. But I never doubted for a minute that I loved him as much as ever. It was all I could think about for weeks. I hadn't really adjusted to the situation when I learned that Andrew, too, was gay. That hit me pretty hard because then I realized that Hjordy and Paul would probably never be grandparents. If there was ever a couple that would be good grandparents, it is them. They would never know the feeling of love that I had holding their two sons.

As for the boys, it never crossed my mind to treat them any different or love them any less. They are our grandsons, and I believe God had a reason for having them different from most other boys. Not everyone would agree with me, but that is a problem they have to work out. The Bible is interpreted in many ways by people much more intelligent than I am. No one knows the answers, but someday we'll all find out. Both boys were brought up in the church, and they carried what they learned into adulthood.

Brad received an award at his graduation that is only given to one graduate each year. It was for helping others. He still continues to help others in so many different ways.

I talked to Andrew not long ago, and he told me that he thanks God every day for five things he is grateful for. What a great idea! More people should do that along with their prayers.

At this point in my life (I'm in my eighties), both boys have very good jobs, and I am very proud of them. But more important, they both have good partners. I love their partners, and I am Grandma to them. Now that I have lost my husband, family is even more special to me. Once in a while, I think how much I would have missed out on if I had taken a different approach to gay people. My grandsons call me, e-mail me, and visit me when they can. I am a very lucky grandma to have them in my life!

*—Grandma*

# PART IV

## TOOLS FOR NAVIGATING YOUR OWN STORY

# Quotes We Live By

*Don't ask of someone else what you are not willing to do yourself.*

Could I ignore my love for my husband (wife) if I were told I couldn't be with him (her)? That judgment is passed on to homosexual couples all the time by people's comments, looks, and by the laws of our country.

*It's important to do what is right, not just what is easy.*

In the beginning, we did what was easy—we hid in our closet. That closet is a lonely and dark place. We now feel we are doing the right thing. It is so much nicer out in the sunshine.

*Wouldn't it be a great world when we judge others by whom they are inside rather than a label?*

Nothing changed inside our sons when they told us they were gay except they were happier they told us. We loved them before, and we love them now because of who they are inside.

*Life is about moments—make your moments count for something.*

When confronted with the big deals in life, it is important to select the right words. People remember those moments for years to come. Make your words count.

*The perfect world is what we seek; the imperfect world is what we live in.*

We know we are all imperfect. Striving to improve, to listen, and to learn is how we get a little closer to the perfection we strive for on a daily basis.

*Got to be taught before it is too late. (from South Pacific)*

We cannot take too much time to learn that which we don't understand—there is too much to lose if we don't. Look at what you may miss in a loved one's life. And more tragically, maybe they will give up their life if despair drains their spirit.

*God knew you before you were born; no one is a mistake. (Quote by Desmond TuTu)*

That says it all. These are words to live by. We are what we are by design.

# Tips for Parents and Friends: How to respond when a friend or loved one comes out

- ✓ Take a deep breath and be thoughtful. Your initial response to your son, daughter, niece, nephew, or friend will be long remembered.

- ✓ Body language speaks volumes as it is 50 percent of your communication; tone is 40 percent, with words only 10 percent of your communication. Even though it is a difficult moment, try to keep your body language open and welcoming. Even if you say words that are accepting, your son or daughter will know they aren't sincere if you have *un*accepting body language, such as crossed arms, head shaking, gaze avoidance, sobbing, or scowling. This could be your biggest challenge of the moment.

- ✓ Ask questions that are on your mind. You can't ask anything that they haven't thought about.

- ✓ Always assure them of your love for them. If they feel you think less of them or are disappointed in them, your relationship could take a critical turn.

- ✓ Keep talking. Don't shut down the communication.

# Tips for Children: How to have a positive coming out experience

- ✔ Select a time when there isn't a lot of stress in the family.

- ✔ Select a location that will provide privacy for you and your parents.

- ✔ Answer your family member's questions openly and honestly.

- ✔ Give them time to do their research, to think about this new information, to ask questions, and time to redesign their vision of who you are and what your future will look like.

- ✔ Don't take their initial response too seriously. You have known for some time. This is new information to them, and their initial reaction might not be a true reflection of their ultimate feelings.

- ✔ Keep talking. Don't shut down the communication.

# What Can We Do in Our Schools?

On April 8, 2008, there was a startling newspaper article in our local paper about a middle school health teacher who told her students that she was gay. Students in this teacher's class are allowed to submit any question on their mind at the end of their seventh grade human growth and development class. For years students asked her the question, "Are you gay?" For years she declined to share her response to that personal information. She finally decided it was time to answer the question. She informed her staff and her principal that it was her intention to answer that question. Her principal was present during all of her classes that day.

Some parents were very upset by this announcement and felt it was their right to be informed of this prior to the question & answer day. One thing led to another, and this became a hot topic in the newspaper and on the blogs. We know that middle school students have many questions about a variety of subjects, but the most important questions are those concerning themselves. It is a messy stage of life where parents are no longer number one and friends are everything. They become aware of their newfound attractions that may not have been evident prior to middle school. Health class is one place where they can learn more about themselves and others. It is a safe zone where questions are answered. Because of our own experiences in the school setting and what we read in our local newspaper, the *Leader-Telegram*, and in the blogs, we wrote a letter to the editor regarding this issue.

## LETTER TO THE EDITOR

April 8, 2008

I wasn't shocked to read about (name left out for her protection)'s announcement she is homosexual. Students are curious and want to have answers. There has been little opportunity for them to increase their knowledge and understanding of homosexuality. It has been a "closet discussion" in the schools. Young people talk among others in their age group about who is gay. Homophobic remarks are evident in the hallways; students are in tears as a result of those remarks.

According to "Report on the Secretary's Task Force on Youth Suicide," a 1989 U.S. Department of Health and Human Services study: *"A majority of suicide attempts by homosexuals occur during their youth, and gay youth are 2 to 3 times more likely to attempt suicide than other young people. They may comprise up to 30 percent of (the estimated 5,000) completed youth suicides annually."*

*The report recommended that "mental health and youth service agencies can provide acceptance and support for young homosexuals, train their personnel on gay issues, and provide appropriate gay adult role models; schools can protect gay youth from abuse from their peers and provide accurate information about homosexuality in health curricula; families should accept their child and work toward educating themselves about the development and nature of homosexuality"*

These recommendations were done in 1989. What advances have been made in Eau Claire? The time has come to open the closet door and give students a chance to learn and understand what homosexuality is and isn't. (Teacher's name) has done her part as suggested in this report. She is an appropriate role model and she is providing information. Students in this age group are currently vulnerable to receive inaccurate information resulting in inappropriate behaviors and perpetuation of inaccuracies. Support of her efforts and all recommendations contained in the federal report should be called for—not condemned.

*—Paul & Hjordy Wagner*

Based on the recommendations found in the 1989 report and the recent incident at this middle school, we created a checklist for educators. What better place to educate our youth on this diversity issue?

# Checklist for Educators

Discriminatory policies and attitudes that persist in our schools and workplaces are hurtful to GLBT people and their loved ones. Children in our schools and adults in our workplaces should be free to live their life openly and without discrimination. Based on our observations in the school and workplace setting, we would make the following recommendations for educators.

- ☐ Check with your school district to see what policies and procedures are in place to protect GLBT students and staff.

- ☐ Check with your school district to see what support services are provided for GLBT students and staff members.

- ☐ Review the list of written resources available to students in the counselor's office as well as the school library.

- ☐ Request staff development offerings to sensitize school staff on GLBT issues. Awareness is the first step to understanding.

- ☐ Check with PFLAG (Parents and Friends of Lesbians & Gays) through their web site (www.pflag.com) to see if there is a chapter within your region where GLBT students or staff members can seek assistance.

☐ Check online resources such as The Rainbow Connection, found at www.the-rainbow-connection.org, that provides support and stories to help families of GLBT and their families. This, along with PFLAG online, is a valuable resource.

☐ Consult with counselors regarding personal or student-related GLBT issues. They are bound by confidentiality and trained to deal with issues that affect staff members and students.

☐ Purge the term *gay* from your vocabulary and that of others when it is used in a degrading manner. Phrases often heard in the hallways of the schools are, "That's gay" or "You're gay." Teachers need to be proactive in speaking with students about the use of that phrase and the harm it causes to a potentially gay student or staff member.

☐ Avoid the water cooler jokes and lounge talk about homosexuals. This is true in any workplace setting and in the classroom. You never know who may be gay in your audience or who has a loved one who is gay.

☐ Speak up when something offensive is said about homosexuals. This is true in the classroom, the lounge, the school hallway, at social events, and at home. Sometimes people say things without realizing the implications.

☐ Avoid stereotyping what girls and boys should do. Remarks such as "sissy" or "tomboy" have negative connotations.

As we said in the preface, we cannot ask gay teachers and gay children to hide in the closet because they are afraid of harassment, bullying, or job security. Some positive changes have been made in the schools and workplace, but there is still a lot of work to be done.

# Dear Abby Speaks Out

On Tuesday, March 25, 2008, a Dear Abby letter appeared in our local paper, the *Leader-Telegram*. The title of the article was, "Parents Should Hear How Gay Son Struggled." The reader described dating a man who later confessed to her that he was gay. He never told his parents he was gay because he feared their reaction. He had observed them snicker about gays and indicated to the reader that his parents felt being a homosexual wasn't normal. Overcome by depression, the young man committed suicide. The mother blamed the girlfriend. After all, if she hadn't broken up with him, he wouldn't have become depressed and taken his life. The reader wanted to know if she should tell his parents the truth.

Abby responded to the reader that she should tell the man's parents he was gay and that his depression stemmed from his concern over how his parents would react to having a homosexual son. She further warned that it probably wouldn't change the parent's view of the situation and they would continue to blame the young woman.

This incident reinforces the need for education on this diversity issue. As we said in the preface, we cannot afford to lose one more child through suicide because he or she is homosexual.

# Paul's Top Ten List

Dad's reflections were organized by his top ten list of things to do after a loved one has revealed they are homosexual. The main categories have been recapped here for quick reference.

10. Have an open mind

9. Get educated

8. Practice tolerance

7. Don't burn bridges

6. Be a good listener

5. Be nonjudgmental

4. Pray

3. Show your support on issues

2. Put yourself in their shoes

1. Look to the future

# What Is **Your Story?**

We would like to share *your* story in a follow-up book. The intent is to create a resource for others to share their story about a gay or lesbian family member or friend.

All you have to do is send us your story; an e-mail with a word attachment containing your story is all we need. We will edit it, if necessary, and bring these excerpts together into a follow-up book.

Our hope with this book and any book to follow is to help you see that you are not alone. People around the world face this at some time in their life with a friend or relative. We pray this will help you through your own experiences in the past, present, or future. Part V of this book is a preview from friends who have shared their story with us. We hope to hear from you.

E-mail your story to us: readyornotstories@gmail.com

# PART V

## STORIES FROM OTHERS

# Crystal Clear

*"I was so grateful Brad had risked the
conversation and heard that God's love
embraced him just as he was, for who he was."*

I was working in my office the day Brad came to see me. He had something he wanted to discuss with me.

The "verbatim" escapes me. The heart of the conversation is crystal clear to me to this day.

Most of us have those moments that wash over us when we wonder if we've made any contribution to the common good while we've lived on this earth. I've spent twenty-three years in full-time pastoral ministry. Every so often, those doubts pull at me. And when that happens, my conversation with Brad some years ago consistently comes back to me.

Brad told me he was gay. I told Brad he was a beloved child of God. Brad told me he was gay. I told Brad his sexuality is a gift of God and can be lived out faithfully and in healthy ways.

We talked about a number of related things: meeting other gay men in safe, healthy ways; the importance of his education; coming out to his parents and to other family and friends; the sense of isolation he might experience. I thought I could feel Brad relax a bit and breathe more easily as we talked. Maybe it was just the relief that our conversation had not confirmed his fears. I was so grateful Brad had risked the conversation and heard that God's love embraced him just as he was, for who he was.

From time to time it seems like we do the very right thing. 100 percent right.

That was my conversation that day with Brad. 100 percent right that he recognized his spiritual self was intertwined with this sexuality. 100 percent right that his self-understanding was affirmed. The heart of that conversation is crystal clear for me to this day.

Brad has been, and continues to be, a gift to me. I have been blessed.

*—Rev. Janet Ellinger*
*River Falls United Methodist Church*

# Not One but TWO!

*"My kids are both so incredibly tolerant of differences that they are my constant teachers."*

October 16, 1981, was perhaps the most joyous day of our five years together as a couple; it was the day our son Matt was born. Matt was a very happy and contented baby. His joy of life and ours increased on April 7, 1983, when his sister Stephanie was born. Both children are intelligent, physically beautiful, creative, and kind. They have been best friends from the start and sources of constant joy for Steve and me throughout their lives.

The first time we heard the word "gay" associated with Matt was when he was two years old; he had picked out a red, heart-shaped purse at a garage sale that he loved to carry around filled with blocks and other treasures. We thought it was adorable, but his paternal grandfather expressed concern that our allowing him to carry the purse might make him gay. The next time was when he came home from the first grade at age six and asked me what "gay" meant. The boys at school were calling him "gay," and he wanted to know what they meant. I told him that the word gay has two meanings in our society, one meaning is a happy and lighthearted person and the other is a person who is attracted to members of the same gender. Matt definitely preferred girls as friends so immediately stated, "I am gay because I am a lighthearted and happy person." I told him he sure was, which made him feel very happy and content; it wasn't until the next day when he responded to the taunts with the same enthusiastic affirmation that the problems began.

The taunting continued throughout his grade school and middle school years; there were many times that we had to console our crying child who was being rejected and bullied by many of the boys in his school. We watched as our child, who once shone like the sun, lose some of his light and become withdrawn and defensive. He always had our full support and knew his home was a safe haven. Throughout his childhood he would often ask us if we thought he was gay. We would respond that it was really too early to tell since he was not attracted in a romantic way to either girls or boys at his age. We assured him that it made no difference to us whether he was gay or not and to know our love for him was not dependent upon that issue.

During sixth grade we were forced to go to the school to address the bullying. Matt was being tripped, pushed, and punched in the hallways. He said teachers were often present but never seemed to notice. The crowning touch was one day when he came home from school very upset because the physical education teacher had encouraged the other boys on the softball field to taunt him when he got up to bat. Saying Matt played like a girl and could not hit, the teacher told all the boys to move into the infield. Now, for some boys and girls, this taunting might prompt them to hit the ball out of the park, which might have been the teacher's thinking (but I doubt it). Matt struck out to the jeering and taunting of his classmates. My husband and I went the next day to launch a complaint. The bullying and taunting were minimized as "boys will be boys," but the principal and counselor said they would speak with all of the teachers and the physical education instructor regarding the issues. The teacher was later dismissed for sexual harassment of another student. Matt said nothing changed at school; he now only felt safe walking through the elementary school corridors that adjoined the middle school to walk home, so he did not have to meet up with other boys on the street. We tried to get him into the neighboring school district but were not allowed to do so. We considered home schooling, but Matt did not want to be away from his friends…so he persevered.

I do not want to paint a picture of a totally lonely boy. Matt did have many friends. Most of them were girls, but he also had a few boy friends. He is a funny, kind, and creative person, helpful to the teachers and a very good student.

Once in high school, the taunting escalated. Matt often had gum thrown into his hair in the lunchroom, his faced shoved into drinking fountains in the hallway, and open, verbal gay taunts shouted at him in the halls and classrooms. His grades began to fall, and he became fairly depressed. We started him in counseling to help him through this difficult time. Matt started to act out with smoking and drinking and other bad behaviors at school. He was caught with a bottle of Peach Schnapps at a school function and arrested and suspended from school for three days. The irony of the situation was he brought the Peach Schnapps to show he was like everyone else; the fact that he brought Peach Schnapps further proved he was not a "guy." So not only did he get into legal trouble but the taunting increased. Steve and I once again went to the school to explain the bullying he was enduring as well as to express our concern for his mental and physical safety. He was allowed to go on the school trip following our meetings with his sincere promise that it would not happen again. On several occasions he received harassing phone calls at home. When we would get on the line, the boys would continue. They were so sure they had the right to treat someone this way.

When Matt was sixteen, he joined the Eau Claire Children's Theatre and took part in several productions. He started to feel pretty good about himself. That year, on National Pride Day, he came out to us and to the world. We were not surprised by his announcement, but I have to admit my fear for him increased. Sometime around his coming out time was the murder of Matthew Shepard. Although we all felt pretty good about his announcement, we also knew the rest of the world might not. I called my family and told them that Matt had come out and we were very supportive of him. All of the members of my family supported him. Because Steve's parents had expressed negative feelings many times about gays, Matt and Steve did not feel comfortable making an announcement to them. We finally told them three years later. They "loved the sinner but not the sin" at first but have come to accept Matt for who he is. We are all grateful that we did not encounter any of the hateful things that many gays have to endure from family.

After coming out in high school, Matt became a hero of sorts to the other closeted gay kids who thought he was extremely brave to be "out" and put up with the harassment. Some of the "straight" kids at school also respected him for being open and stopped harassing him. The fact that he grew to over six feet tall probably had an effect as well. His last year of school in Altoona was one of his best; he was popular, happy, and got better grades.

Matt moved to Minneapolis to be in a more supportive community and has lived there for the past six years. He has a good job and many friends, both gay and straight. He remains a big part of our lives. He has expressed many times that he is so grateful to have us as parents, as many of his friends were rejected by their parents or they fear rejection so strongly that they lie to their families about their sexuality. It is very difficult to live a lie.

About three years ago, our twenty-two-year-old daughter, Stephanie, told us she too is gay. We were surprised by this announcement because she had dated many boys prior to this. I admit feeling a little disappointed at the time, mostly because of my own lost expectations, but she is in the best relationship of her life with her partner, Alyssa. She and Alyssa live in Chicago, have a nice apartment overlooking Lake Michigan, and are "parents" to four loving cats. Alyssa's family has accepted Stephanie, as we have accepted Alyssa as a part of our family. They are both very fortunate to have the love and support of so many. They plan on having children together in the future. We see another adventure in tolerance from our society.

When Stephanie told me she was in a relationship with Alyssa, I asked her if this was a new feeling for her. I was somewhat confused because I was now very sure that being gay is not a choice but a genetic predisposition. It seemed that she was making a choice to be gay. She admitted that she had always felt more strongly attracted to girls, but since Matt had come out she did not want to seem to be following in her brother's footsteps once again, so had kept her feelings inside.

Our families are supportive and have invited Alyssa to family functions without reservation. Matt has not had a sustained relationship to date. The striking difference that I see is in how lesbians are more accepted or ignored in our society than are gay men. Two women can cozy up to each other in public, hold hands, and even kiss without anyone taking note, but two men acting the same way would be stared at by most and publicly ridiculed and harassed by many.

I had a friend ask me what the odds were of having two gay children. I thought it was an odd question. I would now answer that it is about as odd as having two blue-eyed children. I am also asked what it's like to be a parent of gay children. My answer? There is no difference. As children, they were bright, happy, loving, creative, playful, moody, naughty, helpful, unhelpful—everything all children are. As adults, they continue to be happy, loving, creative, and moody just as they were as children. In other words—perfectly human.

I recently heard of someone's idea to use genetic markers to determine sexual orientation before birth, giving prospective parents the option of aborting a possibly gay child. I became so saddened by the possibility that someone would choose not to let people like my children live because they have a genetic marker for homosexuality. What a loss; what a waste.

I am grateful to have had the experience of having gay children; I have learned so much about our society, my own ideas of intolerance, and my capacity to change any prejudice I may have harbored. My kids are both so incredibly tolerant of differences that they are my constant teachers. As a family, we are all working to change society's perception of gay, lesbian, bisexual, and transgender people as well as all other differences. We feel it is our duty and responsibility to perhaps pave an easier road for these children in the future. Viva la difference.

—*Kay Peterson*
*Altoona, Wisconsin*

# My Sister Confided in Me

---

*"She knew that she was gay, but felt like she could not tell anyone, especially her family, for fear of being turned away."*

---

My sister, Kellie, was born while I was in college. We are about twenty years apart in age, so I wasn't around a lot when she was growing up. She is the youngest of five children and was the only child at home while growing up. Mom and Dad were retired for most of the time she was home. They traveled a lot in an RV in the summers. In essence, she was raised as an only child.

In school, Kellie was an excellent student, driven to do her very best. She was involved in some sports and was an excellent drummer in the school band. She also played broomball with her friends for fun. Kellie is a very active person and has always had a huge circle of friends.

During college, she worked hard and was very busy with her female friends. Kellie dated a little, but later told me that in middle school all of her friends were chasing boys and she just never felt a part of that. She did go to prom in high school.

After college graduation, Kellie got a job almost immediately and dated a man for quite some time. This relationship was a turning point in her life. She really tried to make it work, but she couldn't commit totally to the relationship and it broke off. After that she did some soul searching, but became noticeably depressed. She knew that she was gay, but felt like she could not tell anyone, especially her family, for fear of being turned away. My parents, especially my father, were very conservative, and Kellie knew that he would never accept her as being gay. One of my sisters and I were very concerned about this continuing depression. We decided to confront her about what was bothering her. We told her we would not leave until she told us what was going on in her life that made her so unhappy. Kellie finally revealed to us that she was gay. We told her we loved her and accepted her for who she was. We also promised not to tell anyone in the family except our spouses.

Kellie had a few relationships with women and then met a special person. They bought a house together telling everyone that Kellie had bought the house and she needed help with expenses. They came together at holidays and other family gatherings. My parents loved this other person not knowing that this was Kellie's partner. After our father died, Kellie and her partner decided to go through a commitment ceremony and show their love to the world. That meant telling the other family members about their gay relationship. When my brother was told, he said that he had already figured it out. My oldest sister and her husband became upset that they were the last to be told and didn't totally accept Kellie and her partner. They had been known to make unbecoming comments about gay people and were embarrassed that they might have made comments around Kellie. When Kellie told our mother, she asked that my other sister and I be there as support for her and our mother. We weren't really sure how Mom would react. Mom accepted Kellie with open arms.

I took Mom home with me that night so that she wouldn't be alone and had someone to talk with. All weekend Mom would bring up the subject and said she was glad that Kellie had talked with her, but didn't want any of the extended family to know. She is Catholic and knew that many relatives would not accept Kellie. After she went back home, however, Mom became troubled by a lot of questions. What made Kellie gay? When did she know? Why hadn't she told Mom earlier?

Kellie and her partner decided to celebrate their union with a marriage ceremony, just as a marriage is celebrated between a man and a woman. Mom had a lot of trouble with the openness of the marriage. My oldest sister and her husband couldn't understand why they couldn't go on living together quietly like they had been instead of announcing it to the world. This continues to be a source of tension in the family.

Kellie is very open about her sexuality and very happy with her relationship. She continues to be successful in her career and friendships.

*—Judy Brase*
*Red Wing, Minnesota*

# How I Found My Way
## to a Loving Relationship

---

*"I have come to understand that God is*
*available to us all just as we are."*

---

My spiritual journey as it interwove with being gay started before
I knew it. Several memories from my youth have stayed with me.

In the Wisconsin Synod Lutheran church my family belonged
to, confirmation was a junior high experience. Our Saturday-morn-
ing attendance was expected, and we carpooled with the pastor to a
small community served by our church, meeting other soon-to-be
confirmands for two hours of instruction during the course of two
school years. We were to sit still, not eat candy, and be prepared
with our memorized work, knowing we could be called upon at any
time. We snuck candy from time to time, wrote a few notes to one
another, and performed our speaking pieces with various levels of
pastoral satisfaction. These qualities did not seem particularly un-
reasonable to me then, or now, except to my recollection there was
no open-ended dialogue on issues of biblical importance. We were
there to learn what was right and wrong, learn right and wrong the
"right" way, and to only ask questions that would lead to the right
answers. Probing for meaning or considering alternate viewpoints
was not part of the program. Given we were being told the "right"
answers and how to think, I was particularly concerned about my
best friends in school who were Catholic. Right and wrong were
sometimes stated in contrasting beliefs to what my friends suppos-
edly believed, and I was told that their beliefs would have grave

eternal consequences. I didn't understand why God would be like that. To me it wasn't their fault they grew up in a family who had the tradition of being Catholic.

Confirmation classes came to a close, and we were all to make individual commitments to our faith and our church. I wasn't sure which one was of higher emphasis. I thought it wasn't appropriate to ask us as young teens to make any kind of life-binding decision, let alone one that seemed to have something to do with eternity. Maybe my peers could commit genuinely, but I knew I wasn't ready. There was no discussion of whether we wanted to make this commitment, no discussion on the timeline that it could happen, if at all, and no known precedence for a youth actively refusing this rite of passage, something my passive and observational nature would have found tremendously difficult to do anyway. I remember sitting in front of church in my white gown, shoes I hated, and thinking I was stuck. While I don't remember now whether I considered talking with my parents about my reservations, our past communication would have suggested that this supposed faith step was nonnegotiable.

I also remember in my early teens wondering why the sermons seemed like history lessons, and almost always just history lessons. I thought, if Paul and other biblical characters had such important Christian lives, then what's the connection to the rest of us? Is there something that these stories are supposed to be leading us to? Can we talk about that? Is it only about making disciples of all nations? I hardly get to leave my home on a farm, let alone travel the world.

At the supper table as a senior in high school, I announced that one of my term papers was going to be on the job discrimination that some people face as a result of being gay. I thought it was wrong that someone could be fired over this, even though they may be excellent at their work. My mother sharply responded that I would pick a different topic. When asked why, there was no discussion. End of story. My dad said nothing.

Looking back at high school and junior high, I had some feelings and thoughts that I now associate as being my early gay affections. My first conscious awareness of these feelings, however, was during my freshman year at a state college. And it hit me like a ton of bricks.

In my residence hall there was a woman I was getting to know whose qualities and presence won my attention. She lived a few rooms away and was a year ahead of me, like most of my nearest hall mates. She took an approach to life that was full and rich, put herself in risk-taking situations for the growth of it, and spoke with such depth and care about her mother and younger brother. (Her father had left the family years earlier.) This woman was someone I wanted to spend more time with. I rarely had things to say when I'd visit in her room. My life wasn't exciting; all I did was study, and I was rather shy. Making conversation wasn't easy for me, and I felt like I had little to offer her. She, on the other hand, made me feel a different kind of alive just by being around her. I tried to keep visits short, not wanting to overstay any welcome, and I remember it being difficult to make myself leave her room.

I remember one morning awakening very startled by a dream. She was in it and my face had been buried in her bare breasts. Awake, I was stunned. I hadn't had sexual dreams before or spent time thinking about such things. Call me a late bloomer, but my mind had always phrased my affections and interests in people in other ways—feeling deep care, having complete concern, seeing tremendous qualities, identifying impeccable standards, etc. I also felt caught in a double standard—one that put me on the short end of what seemed like a sad predicament.

My personal revelation may have begun that morning, but it clearly was a process. I always felt there must be some misunderstanding of gay people. Certainly they couldn't all be the creepy and immoral people others spoke of them as being. The Church must be missing something because the Church didn't seem to behave very church-like toward these people. Recognizing my physical attraction, however, I felt caught in a hard place. Could I disregard what had just hit me, or must I face the possibility that the label "gay" applied to me? Internally I was jarred. Up to that time, I had never associated my feelings for anyone with a label; they were just feelings of deep care and concern for people who were clearly special in my eyes. These were people who had high standards—people who were kind, down to earth, hardworking, and, in my case, most often female. Sexuality, however broadly or narrowly defined, was never on my mind.

My Christian faith was immediately put on alert. My theoretical standard would have allowed sermons on "other people" to not make sense to me or to seem too harsh, even un-Godlike, but now the thought that I might be one of those people seemed much more threatening. The church, to my knowledge, never explained why gay people were so bad; describing them as "unnatural" was apparently enough to say. Now, as someone who might be among the dammed group, I felt torn about whether to question what I'd heard or just do all I could to escape being gay. While previously I thought there could be some mistake in biblical interpretation and perhaps the Church wasn't able to know about this topic with all certainty, now I felt it inappropriate to question its position since I had something to gain by how that argument turned out. If I was gay, the condemnation I had heard about didn't seem a distant theoretical argument anymore. I was afraid hell might be in my future.

Even as a shy country girl, I longed for someone to share this confusion and problem with. Who could I talk to? It certainly wouldn't be my roommate, who I was not close to and was about as different from me as night and day. My resident assistant was an incredible person whom I thought the world of. I could trust that she would only have my best interests in mind, but she, like so many of my nearest hall mates that I considered as friends, attended weekly Bible studies, was part of a Christian organization on campus, and looked to the Bible for personal growth and guidance. They also were the people I shared a community bathroom with. I had no interest in watching anyone shower or get ready for our classes, just as I wanted no one looking at me. But wouldn't they feel uncomfortable if they thought I was gay or struggling to sort that out? Even worse for me, I thought, they'd change from seeing me as a quiet, respectable, conscientious, overachieving student to an untrustworthy pervert. I was afraid that any positive thing they ever thought about me (or could think about me in the future) would be wiped out. They wouldn't be able to see me for who I am; somehow, everything would change and not for the better. There was no way I would talk with any of them.

At some point, I made an appointment with the campus counseling department. Answering the counselor's version of "What brings you here today?" was no easy task. While physically shaking in my chair, some version of saying, "I have strong feelings for a woman in my dorm," came out. After having to clarify in some way what I meant, I recognized the counselor's moment of understanding: she broke eye contact and did some shifting in her chair. Shit. I'd made a mistake coming here. She seemed as creeped out as I feared for from my friends. I remember nothing more from that appointment other than an offer to make another appointment, something I had no intention of doing.

Several of my hall mates noticed I was more withdrawn than usual. Some asked me what was wrong. My RA also inquired. If only I could believe that they wouldn't discard everything they already knew about me as contradictory evidence to a feared term. Their friendship and their respect meant far too much to me to risk sharing my secret.

My solution would be personal. This can be between God and me, I thought. I will pray this away. Doesn't matter how long it will take. I will pray to not have these feelings for this or any other woman. If my feelings are honestly bad in God's eyes, then He'll help me out and He'll know how earnestly I want this to go away.

Multiple campus Bible groups used language of giving your life to Christ, making a decision to have a personal relationship with Jesus. The leadership of these groups, which I met, implied that it wasn't good enough to have infant baptism; you needed to be born again, and you could do so by inviting Jesus into your heart. Given my need for some eternal assurance and given I was praying multiple times a day to not have the longings I had for this woman, going against my Lutheran-taught background made some sense to me. I hoped that by being born again, my present and eternal states would take care of themselves, and nothing spiritually significant from my baptism would be negated. So during my first college semester, I prayed to have Jesus come into my life and make me the kind of person He wanted me to be. I began attending weekly Bible gatherings pretty regularly. I believed I had opted for the best and most private of solutions. Suicide crossed my mind, and I would have had the means to complete it, but the Church (while not as informed as it needs to be) was not keen on that topic either.

If my freshman year was the initial shock wave about my sexual orientation, my sophomore year began multi-years of aftershock. As a sophomore, I had been praying daily to be the kind of person God wanted me to be and believed that that excluded being attracted to women.

Right in front of me, though, was Linda. She was a residence hall leader with high visibility and a knack for actually living life. She was loved by many people, and she lit up the time and space around her. Her communication skills were strong; she worked to say what she meant, she avoided speaking in generalities, and she held people accountable for the word choices they made. Stereotypes were challenged, negativity was channeled toward constructive activity, and people's strengths were drawn out. She was good at relationship building and developing a residence hall atmosphere that would quickly surpass all others on campus. My mind and heart were awoken again.

My black-and-white thinking that leaked into my language was fair game for Linda's questions. My assumptions of right and wrong and how to apply them to someone else's life (apparently something I felt qualified to do periodically) were identified for what they were: my judgment, usually, my perspective at best. I thought that as we were getting to know one another I could say something followed by, "You know what I mean," and thus be understood. Nope. I was challenged to take responsibility for improving my communication. That was both good and hard. And in the meantime, my heart was melting. She had a laugh and a life about her that made me feel good. She accepted me for who I was, faults and all, and it made me want to be better. To see her live life richly while expecting excellence from herself and others was eye-opening. You can do both? I had seen or experienced excellence before, but it was usually coupled with lots of sacrifice—sleep deprivation, little to no fun, deafening mental discipline.

I felt somewhat practiced at squelching any thought of attraction or interest, though practice had not translated to it becoming easier. Saying no to my internal awareness came from strict mental dialogue. I regularly denied letting my thoughts wander or pursue a personal daydream. Getting to know Linda, however, did a number on my heart. I fell in love with a lesbian woman.

It didn't make sense to me. Why would God be disappointed in me for the things I felt toward her? My desires were of the heart. I wanted what was best for her. I only wanted to be good for her and add in positive ways to her life, if I was capable of that. I wanted her to continue being the healthy influence she was on others, helping people to grow in their communication, and making life better for others. She was both fun and thought-provoking to be with. I felt she had purpose and direction in her life that included God and that was lived out in her interactions with others. I didn't have thoughts and feelings that if spoken aloud would be condemned by good people. My feelings were not creepy or perverted or lustful. To wish to be close to her, to want to hold hands, to spend time talking or not talking, to observe and learn what good communication is, to have my limited view of life challenged and to still be loved anyway—these were the things that I craved, and I craved them from her. And in some measure, these are the things that I received over the two years we lived in the same hall.

I was convinced that if I shared my feelings about her to others by trying to describe her as "him," how he made me feel, how I felt toward him, how I only had good and pure hopes for him, that all my listeners would be excited and thoughtfully supportive of my growing love. My friends and any campus Bible study leader or pastor would smile and assure me that what I was describing was a love from God. If I could have put words to the qualities and effects he had on those around him, pastors of various faiths and my family would say he's a keeper, and they would be so pleased for me in finding and participating in such a love. They would want to meet him and see us interact together. They would come to the conclusion of wanting to see our love and relationship at some point blessed through a long-term commitment to one another. This would be a version of heaven on earth. This would be, of course, if he was a he. And it wouldn't be any of these things for these people if he was a she.

It broke my heart. I laid in bed at night, night after night, crying and praying myself to sleep. My questions were over and over again, how could God be disappointed with this? How could He really mean this deserves hell? What sense does this make?

My internal dialogue played both sides. I was aware of a passage that God is the potter and we are the clay, and as such, He could throw away any pot He wants to. But why? Why, when the qualities identified are so positive and the feelings that exist reverberate so purely, could it all be for nothing due to gender? If God is God, I would fight with myself, He can do anything He wants, including things that don't make sense. I would remind myself that it doesn't make sense that a blameless Jesus would die on the cross for us to somehow pay for our sins, even ones we haven't committed yet. Certainly it doesn't make sense that people who didn't grow up in a nation exposed to Christianity would have hell as their eternity. How could God doom people of faraway countries to hell because some of us don't follow through on his "make disciples" command? No, my heart would cry. This isn't right.

Right versus wrong is a hard way to view life. My experiences operated from that view. My orientation to the world was in black-and-white terms. My family influence and my early church influence formed that perspective in me, and there was no realm of my life that it did not affect. Additionally, no contrasting influences suggested that right versus wrong might be relative to where one was cast in life. Or that life would be a series of choices that are rarely all good or all bad. Not until I met Linda, that is.

My nightly dialogue of questions continued, and I prayed for answers. I so badly wanted to know if my anguish and denial were required of me to develop in God's image. Given I had no answers to my "why" questions, I gravitated toward a probability approach to my dilemma. Math was a strong suit of mine during school. It was natural for me to think in mathematical terms at times, so now didn't seem oddly different. It started like this.

I knew my feelings and desires to be pure and as wholesome as any I'd ever felt. I also believed the Bible might and many churches did condemn these same feelings. Could we be misinterpreting the Bible, or is God really serious that hell would be the outcome? What if there's a 50 percent chance that we've misinterpreted the Bible (my feelings are okay, maybe even Godly) and a 50 percent chance that God says no (my feelings are not acceptable)? What should I do? Can I take a 50 percent chance, knowing that if I'm wrong, eternity looks really bad? I cried and committed myself in prayer to not take that chance.

I went next to 60:40. The 60 percent was, What if that handful of verses got messed up? Clearly there are different translations, and how can we really know? It's senseless to condemn my heartfelt care and concern for this woman, but (the 40 percent) if He's said it's wrong, it's wrong. Forty percent chance of something this important isn't trivial. This isn't a sliver. It could happen. Through tears and a heavy heart, I committed to not taking that chance.

My internal debate forged on. I remember being more concerned about Linda's eternity than my own. Sometimes I reminded myself that my own eternity was at stake too.

Seventy:thirty came next. What if the traditional stance on this topic has landed in the wrong place? What if God really doesn't care about the gender of a person so long as the love shared between them is patient and kind, forbearing and forgiving, holding one another to high standards and always supporting and encouraging one another? Or, what if this is just something we're not supposed to ask questions about and instead just accept as being unacceptable? My mind would argue that 70 percent acceptable is more than twice as much as 30 percent unacceptable. I don't know how many nights went by before coming to my decision. If I really claim to love her, I told myself, then I can't take this chance.

The pace of my probability debate slowed. My nightly prayer would resume where the previous night's had left off. I was now at 75:25. God thinks it's fine, God has no problem, God would be disappointed, even, to have believers stand in the way of other believers who find true happiness and profound love with the same gender. Or, we don't get to understand everything, we aren't the rule makers, I'm just a pot, don't play God. This is 3:1. This scenario is in my favor. But what if I'm wrong? What if I'm wrong? I love Linda too much to take this chance.

My feelings and my probability quest continued. If a mind can pace, mine was doing it. This was a hell of a way to go to sleep at night. My 80:20 version came next. Same arguments, different tears, same outcome. I remember being in a fetal position and burying my head in covers during one of these number scenarios. At some point there was 85:15, and then 90:10. Arriving at personal decisions each time was mandatory in my soul. I knew I loved Linda with the best of what love can be. If I really love her, how could I put her in harm's way? In anguish I proceeded to 95:5 and later 99:1. Images of a needle in a haystack were present. I've seen haystacks up close and personal. Out of that entire mound, every stick but one says, it's okay with God. My voice inside screamed, How can this be wrong? In response, the alternate voice said, it just is. My possibility of exploring a relationship was turned down.

For five years I prayed with regularity to not feel what I felt, to instead be the kind of person God wanted me to be, and with rare exception, I removed myself from situations that felt tempting in some way. I stayed clear of places where I knew some gay women congregated. I avoided a building where lots of the female athletes had classes or met one another. (Only some of them were gay, of course.) I told myself "no" when an exchange with a female classmate or hall mate sent a tingle through me. As for Linda, I continued to love her but chose to "show it" by keeping some distance. I remained in her life when she left campus and at times tried through letters and occasional phone calls to encourage her to give up her gay feelings for others. My motivation was out of real love for her. It pained me that a relationship with a woman wasn't something she believed needed to be avoided for her eternal safety. Here I had made what for me was the ultimate sacrifice and it might not do her any good anyway.

During this span I completed my undergraduate work. I would finish a double major in microbiology and biology with minors in chemistry and math before heading to Madison, Wisconsin, for work in a pharmaceutical laboratory. My work benefited from my "do it right" approach, and I was soon identified as one of the better protocol followers and analytical report writers. I poured myself into work and had little social life other than writing a few important college friends.

Now, some nine or more years after my initial awareness of same-gender attraction, I so badly wanted a clear sign of God's acceptance of my gay feelings, one that would allow my love to venture into the option of a relationship, that I would pray for a miraculous sign.

I knew I could attend various churches until I found a message that "suited" me. The Yellow Pages offered numerous advertisements for churches like I'd grown up in and others that expressly stated their acceptance of GLBT people. I attended both types. I attended other Christian churches as well, feeling somehow traitor-like guilt in relation to my upbringing. Regardless of the words said in any of them, I was uncomfortable in all of them. Finding a church that said what I longed to hear didn't seem to me like finding God's truth. It felt more like shopping for comfort. While I now wouldn't discount the value of finding comfort as part of one's spiritual journey, it was the truth that I sought and needed. To me, truth was set; it wasn't malleable or potentially pluralistic. To trust truth at that time, I needed it to come directly from God and in an unmistakable form.

I prayed for a specific and an unmistakable sign. Bible study had taught that prayer should be specific. So I prayed to have the cast-iron fry pan (hanging on a wall in my living room next to a Boundary Waters guide map) fall on my head while I slept in an adjacent room, precisely in a manner so that I'd awaken to see in a mirror the imprint of the skillet size from its bottom surface, placed squarely on my large forehead. Really! While I knew this to be an absurd and most unlikely answer to prayer, it represented how desperately I wanted no mistake in understanding God's "it's okay" message for me. I did not want to screw up with the potential love of my life, let alone in a way that would bring condemnation. It would require God's, and only God's, intervention to make that impression, and it would only be Godly intervention that I believed I could trust.

My longing for blessings on my love for another woman demanded God prove that gayness was not contrary to his intentions for me or others. Though any scrap of acceptance would have been nice, I opted for a high level of proof. A major headache to pound His point home would have been just fine with me. Unfortunately, the black skillet never fell, nor did it fly across the apartment to knock me on my head.

How I went from requiring proof to letting this issue have some kind of hiatus is less vivid to me in comparison to the painful memories of constant denial. While I don't blame anyone for how I decided to handle my personal awareness of being gay, I know I was profoundly impacted by messages from the church of my upbringing, the perception that most churches perpetuate the idea that gay is wrong, and the lack of positive gay images in society. I know I wore down mentally and emotionally and just couldn't dedicate such single-minded focus toward regulating me anymore. My questions still had no better answers. With no one within reach as a potential person for a relationship, it also seemed like wasted hyper-vigilance. While I still loved Linda deeply and had remained in contact with her, the years of separate direction and having different energy levels toward life meant we would always be dear to one another but not a couple. And while I had grown quite fond of Steph, a younger college friend, she didn't know I was gay or that she was gay. My feelings for her didn't particularly need rectifying. I was sticking to myself.

As time went on, my analytical bent remained strong, but I was becoming aware of its shortcomings. I took life awfully seriously— my work, my faith, my perceived duty to not influence anyone else in a way that might be harmful to him/her. I operated from a do-no-harm perspective. While I'd been told not to be so serious sometimes by a family member, it wasn't delivered with love, so I readily dismissed the advice. A realization of this sort isn't along the lines of deciding to wear brighter clothing from now on. Coming to this conclusion and how to make shifts toward a healthier outlook on life would take years. But its start included awareness of the empty places in my life, like driving home from a day's work and finding no one to share meaningful personal time with.

At work, my singleness appeared to my supervisor that I was more available for an extra project or tight deadline than my married colleagues. There were no kids to pick up from day care daily; there was no special spousal event preventing me from staying late. It wasn't that I wanted a personal life to get out of work. I had little problem working hard or late, but I sometimes resented that my colleagues benefited from my marital status. Or maybe it's that they benefited from theirs. Having only work and society's substandard acceptance of singlehood weren't filling me up. My life of denial, a life without the option of personal love, was emotionally draining. Feeling whole was not my experience. Life wasn't abundant.

Somehow I began considering different questions than those of my earlier mantra.

Now it was wondering, how could God be pleased by my denial of unselfish love? How can feeling emotionally flat and empty because of gender be right or make God proud? Who or what says living life must be based on one's head without considering the messages of the heart? If we're made in God' image, why would we disregard the mental and emotional health discoveries of the twentieth century? Are the only things of importance the ones revealed two thousand years ago, and thus nothing since then counts?

I had been living out of fear. Living out of fear, rather than joy or love or abundance or gratitude, was the lens I was filtering life through. Where did that come from? Was some unhealthy communication of my youth a factor? Was hearing everything pitted against one another as either good or bad a factor? Might a literal interpretation of the Bible set this in motion? And how can literal biblical interpretation be more worthy for understanding God and His interests for our lives than contextual interpretation?

These kinds of questions began surfacing over time, not in a raging sort of way, but such that they made me question my earlier approach. Maybe I'd spent too much time asking the wrong questions and thus coming up with decisions that picked away at my soul, disregarding the feelings and emotional capacity that God gave me, too. If we have to live with unanswered questions, then how about living with ones that lead to buoying the spirit, adding life to life, and having emotional energy to reach out to others?

At the end of my undergraduate days, I was introduced to golf in completion of a physical education requirement. The sport and I meshed rather well. My long levers were coachable, and my mind enjoyed the physics and demeanor of the game. I visited golf courses in Madison and got asked to sub on a women's league. After accepting many sub requests, the next year's vacancy allowed me to sign on as a regular. I met some nice people and became golf buddies with several of them. Any kind of topic can come up when walking between holes in a foursome or pair—family, relationships, work, etc. Work was the safest for me, though using layman's terms to describe it translated to a short description that I repeated with regularity to whoever asked. Family and relationships were land mine topics, so being brief and nondescript, particularly in relation to gender and names, felt safest. Tending to be more of a listener, I didn't prattle on about some topics and then get mysteriously quiet about personal life. When you're gay, you learn quickly how to filter language to maintain boundaries, whether someone else's or your own. Work, golf, and keeping in touch with a few college friends occupied my time. One such friend was Steph, whom I met through a Bible study my last semester.

Steph's coming-of-age process was different than my own in relation to spirituality but had in common the aspect of being an adult process over time. While I felt a unique draw toward her from the beginning, it would be years before she independently determined her capacity to love a woman. My thoughts early on aligned with either having her as a friend or not having her at all. A friend sure sounded better and became my decision. Time taught me that a discrepancy in affection levels can be more challenging than initially bargained for. But later when friendship hinted toward a relationship, my growing sense of healthier spiritual questions came into play. We avoided talking about our feelings for quite some time. Beyond the elements of sorting through any relationship for its compatibility and support levels, there are hard realities to add when contemplating a relationship that others, without even knowing you, will discredit or worse.

My spirituality knew what a battle it was to wrestle over my sexual orientation and what to do with love for someone of my gender. Over time my heartfelt experiences helped inform my spirituality, or vice versa, as I was coming to believe that God can't be pleased with personal denial that's packed with mental or emotional abuse, no matter who or what the source.

Not knowing how many times a person might get a chance at love, I was not going to let it get away again. After seven years of friendship with Steph that turned into mutual falling in love, we claimed our love as forever to one another, and we have been lifetime partners for thirteen years.

I have learned that there is more to being a balanced and healthy person, a person interested in living with the Divine and interacting with Its creation, than only moving through life on the strengths, and weaknesses, of rational arguments. I believe we are built with intuition, feelings, and orientations to life that need to weigh in on the course of one's life. I didn't have a choice in being gay. I've never met anyone who has said he/she did. My only choice was about how to handle that personal awareness. My story has been one of spending prayerful years trying to change or deny my feelings; that process was wearing to my core. My motive was sincere, but the process was unhealthy.

My partner and I are members of a Methodist church in Eau Claire, Wisconsin. Over the years it has challenged us to grow and live out God's involvement in and through our lives. The denomination is not perfect, but it recognizes that faith is part Scripture, part reason, part tradition, and part experience. While my personal process of determining God's will for my life has had its flaws, I am so thankful not to have confused the Church or Bible study for God. I understand why some people who feel unaccepted by the Church would end up fleeing the Church, and in confusing Church with God, would end up fleeing God. But I have also come to understand that God, The Divine, or any other name for The Sacred, is available to us all just as we are. Thank God.

*—Cheryl Sutter*
*Eau Claire, Wisconsin*

# Connections Matter

*"One of my friends said that you can't fully be yourself when you're closeted because you're lying about a huge part of who you are."*

## Setting the stage...

In preparation for an upcoming event, I focused on really getting my body healthy. The quest eventually led me to join a gym that I wasn't familiar with called The Firm. I was looking to take my working out to the next level, but what resulted from The Firm changed my life more than I could have ever imagined.

My first impression of The Firm was that it was incredibly edgy and trend forward. There is a different feeling, which I experienced the first time I came to The Firm. That feeling comes not only from the aesthetic of the gym but from the demeanor of the teachers, staff, and the people who attend. When I peeled back beyond the outrageous, exciting aerobic classes that were offered, I discovered that The Firm was also a place where people from all walks of life are welcome and you could really be comfortable expressing yourself. For me personally, I was able to be a more outgoing person and get in the best shape of my life. Beyond being a client at The Firm, I was able to connect with one of the instructors there in a big way.

When you first take a class with Brad, you become a "fan" immediately. In addition to being energetic, cool, and charismatic, he makes a big effort to connect with all the students in his class. I admired his passion for making fitness fun, fresh, and for everyone. I knew almost immediately that he was gay, as The Firm has a large population of homosexual, heterosexual members and also people who are discovering who they are in general. I remember thinking, "I want to be friends with him."

Striking up a friendship with Brad takes time, to say the least. It's not like college where you spend large amounts of time with your fellow classmates or live in close proximity. Brad worked for Target, in addition to teaching at The Firm six days week, and I worked for a large company as well. Both of us had demanding jobs and were in very serious relationships. Also, he was my teacher, and getting beyond a teacher-student relationship can take time.

There was a pivotal point in time where our separate personal lives were taking a turn for the worst. I remember being in a tough place during my first few months of being married and going to The Firm to escape if only for an hour a day. One day Brad seemed really sad. He loves to teach and always checks any woes he may have at the door whenever he comes to The Firm so he is there 100 percent for his students. I knew something was wrong. He told me about the tough time he was going through in his personal life, and I remember thinking, "I'm going to be a good friend to him starting right now. No more waiting for it to evolve."

That was two years ago, and I like to think that Brad and I became friends during darker times in our lives and have supported each other as we moved back to the light. The things I learned from him are impossible to quantify, but he was the first gay guy that I really got to know well. He broke down any stereotypes I had about what being a gay man in Minneapolis was like and the life that you lead as a gay man.

## My brother comes to The Firm

It's hard to explain the level of love that a sister has for her one and only brother. It would be the understatement of the century to say that I adore him. Even though we fought as children, since becoming young adults we've always been solid friends, and we champion each other. Throughout his collegiate career, he had been struggling to discover who he really was. He encountered more challenges throughout college and was in a dark time in his life. I encouraged him, along with basically anybody I knew, to check out The Firm. It was a place where you could be yourself and get a great workout. What I didn't expect was that he would embrace it so fully. He spent a lot of time there and made some great friends with a group of guys who all happened to be gay.

He had always told me he was straight, but in my gut I knew he wasn't being honest from a very early time. What was great about The Firm is that it stopped him from feeling alone and not normal. My brother hung with his group of friends beyond the gym, and I started seeing him out at parties where it was mostly gay men and a few women. I knew he was working through his process of discovering who he was, but for some reason I wasn't as prepared as I thought I would be when I got a phone call from him one Sunday evening.

## The most important wake-up call

I remember that I was sleepy and that my brother called me and said he had something important to tell me. He told me he was gay. I woke up quickly. I remember saying how happy I was that he could tell me and that I would support him 100 percent. I think I did a good job because my goal was for him to be free. I know that coming out of the closet is a scary time, and I wanted him to just focus on his new freedom and enjoy it.

Once I go off phone with him, I started thinking about how difficult his life must have been leading up to this and also the adversity that he might face from people who aren't accepting. I also felt guilty that he ever had to be closeted in the first place from me. My ideal is a world where you don't closet yourself ever: during puberty, when we start to think about sex, we would figure it out and just "be" from there. I burst into tears and called Brad. I freaked for a few minutes.

Based on that conversation with Brad, Paul and Hjordy, whom I love because they remind me a little of my parents, sent me the first chapter of the rough draft of their book. Reading about "the first twenty-four hours" was both comforting and upsetting. I was comforted to learn that people get through this process and loved to hear how the person who just came out feels like a massive weight has been lifted off their shoulders. I was upset because the story is about Brad's coming out, and I hated the idea of Brad and his family being upset or pained. Also I knew that my brother hadn't told our parents, so I dreaded what their first twenty-four hours would be like. Every family is different.

Later my brother was able to come out to our parents and some of his friends, but not everyone just yet. It hasn't been easy for him, my parents, or me, but it gets better. I understand that it takes time.

## A new man

My brother is a new man. He's got a light in eyes and a happiness that I've never seen. He's come out of his shell and can be his most authentic self. One of my friends said that you can't fully be yourself when you're closeted because you're lying about a huge part of who you are. Lying about that makes your whole life feel like one big lie. I can see a new honesty in my brother and, most importantly, a sense of freedom. That makes me so happy. I can't wait for us to continue growing together as brother and sister.

## Things I'm thankful for

I'm very thankful that a place like The Firm exists so people can feel comfortable being themselves. I am thankful for Hjordy and Paul, who give me so much hope as to what my parents can be one day. I'm also thankful to them for raising a son who has redefined what friendship can be for me. I'm finally thankful to them for writing this book. This collection of experiences connects us to other human beings who go through the same struggles and victories in a society where it's easy to feel isolated. I think it's one of the most giving things that they could do. It inspires me to give back, pay forward, and ultimately be a better person.

*—Anonymous*
*Minneapolis, Minnesota*

# Gay Lifestyle Just
# Like Everyone Else's

---

*"Being a minority makes one abnormal;
being at the top of one's class does too. It is not
necessarily a bad thing to be abnormal.".*

---

The following special editorial appeared in our local paper, the
*Leader-Telegram*, on August 8, 2008. It is reprinted with the permission of the author, Virginia Wolf, and of the *Leader-Telegram*.

Since last spring I have read letters to the editor in the *Leader-Telegram* about why gay people should keep their lifestyle private. The most recent letter, published July 22, persuaded me to write in the hope that I can explain what all too many seem not to understand. I write from the personal experience of living in a committed same-sex relationship of 33 years.

"Gay lifestyle" is a term used pejoratively by heterosexual people to depict all sexual minorities as promiscuous and sex-driven. Evidence doesn't support this understanding of gay people. There are as many heterosexual people who are promiscuous and sex-driven as there are homosexual people – more, actually, because there are more heterosexual people. If those who want gay people to keep their lifestyle private mean they want them not to talk about sex in public places, I could be a bit more understanding.

The feeling that homosexuality is unnatural arises, I think, because we are a minority, about 10 percent of the population. We once thought racial minorities unnatural, but now we know better. There is homosexuality in the animal world, and we can trace a homosexual presence very far back in history. Writings from ancient Greece, for example, reveal that both gay men and lesbians existed then. If we think of natural as that which exists in nature, homosexuality is natural. If we mean by unnatural that homosexuality is abnormal, then we need to examine what we mean by abnormal. Being a minority makes one abnormal; being at the top of one's class does too. It is not necessarily a bad thing to be abnormal.

More important, in reality, is that a gay person's lifestyle is not any different from anyone else's. We have families and homes and pets and gardens and jobs and churches. And if we keep our lifestyles private, we cannot share as all other people do what our families and lives are like. My life partner and I placed pictures of each other and our kids and our granddaughters all around our desks. We talked about our vacations and other important life experiences we have shared. We refuse to keep everything that is healthy and wonderful about our relationship a secret. We refuse to lie about who we are. Gay people come out because they don't want to live a lie or hide who they are out of fear. Hiding and keeping secrets is not healthy for anyone. Although we always pay some price for coming out in this culture, it is still a relief and a positive experience to be open about who we are.

Finally, there is the issue of same-sex marriage. The government should and can never force churches to perform same-sex marriages. Only those churches who choose to marry gay couples will. This is not a religious issue. The government issues licenses, and judges can officiate at marriages. My point is that there are many benefits (I've read it is over 2,000) that the state and federal government grant to married people. For example, my partner will not get the Social Security benefits that other spouses get. She cannot be on my health insurance, and the list goes on. When our children were young, she could not give permission for an operation our son needed because she was not the biological mother. They had to track me done in Madison where I was attending a conference.

There is no reason why we should not have these benefits or why we should keep our lifestyles private. Think about it, please.

*—Virginia Wolf is minister emerita of the Unitarian Universalist Congregation in Eau Claire, Wisconsin*

# A Look at the Authors

**Paul Wagner:** Paul recently retired from the Eau Claire Area School District after serving as an elementary teacher and elementary physical education spcrialist for thirty-two years. Paul has vast experience writing physical education curriculum, teaching elementary physical education, assisting with workshops for teachers in Wisconsin and Minnesota, and providing consultant services to the Chippewa Valley Montessori School. Paul received his undergraduate degree in physical education and health at Winona State University and an elementary teaching degree and master's degree from the University of Wisconsin Eau Claire.

**Hjordy Wagner:** Hjordy recently retired from the Eau Claire Area School District after thirty-three years of service. She served in several roles over her career, such as elementary and middle school media specialist, district media coordinator, district strategic planner, and district community relations coordinator. She was involved in many local and state boards and committees, including serving on the board and as president of the Wisconsin School Public Relations Association (WSPRA). She is currently managing the Service-Learning grant for the Eau Claire Area School. She continues to be active in WSPRA and local committees in the Eau Claire community. She has written and contributed to professional publications on public relations and local newspaper articles. Hjordy received her undergraduate degree in library/media and speech at Winona State University and a master's degree from the University of Wisconsin Eau Claire. She received specialized training in strategic planning and community relations.

**Brad Wagner:** Brad has been employed at Target Corporation in Minneapolis for the past eleven years where he currently serves as a manager in the Human Resources Department. He volunteers his time by chairing the GLBT Committee for Target Corporation and provides many special aerobic classes for charity. After hours, Brad leads fitness classes at The Firm.

**Andrew Wagner:** Andrew currently resides in Las Vegas, where he works for Hilton Corporation. He graduated from the University of Minnesota, where he received a degree in communications. He is actively involved in personal fitness. Andrew is entrepreneurial and always has projects he is working on to secure his future. Andrew has done some modeling and was featured on the front cover of *Instinct* magazine along with an article entitled, "The Sexiest Guy We Found in Vegas."

*For more information, visit our web site:*
*www.ReadyOrNotStories.com*